WTF is

EBITDA?

A finance primer

WTF is

EBITDA?

A finance primer

(2nd Edition)

Steven Saltman

2nd Edition: Updated in 2025 to fix some things that aren't really very important but were bothering me and add recent examples.

Cover Art: Max Saltman

ISBN: 978-0-9834819-6-6 (2nd Edition)

Library of Congress Control: 2025905963

Finance, Humor, Self-Help

Thanks to my kids, who are awesome.

Contents

This page intentionally and with malice left blank.

Preface

For those who are wondering about the title of this book, here is a quick explanation.

WTF is an initialism[1] for "What The F*(%?." The "F" stands for a well-known naughty four-letter word, and I didn't want to actually write out the entire naughty four-letter word because putting that word in the title of your book isn't a brilliant sales strategy, except for cyber-punk writers, so I used the initialism WTF[2]. Okay, onward...

EBITDA is an acronym that stands for **Earnings Before Interest, Taxes, Depreciation, and Amortization**. It is a financial term that represents a way to measure the profit of a company. It is actually spoken as a word, pronounced ee-bit-dah. Frankly, it sounds kind of silly when spoken, but that's not my fault. If you read this book, you'll know what all those words that make up EBITDA really mean, and you'll be able to bandy about the term EBITDA during casual cocktail party conversation, assuming you engage in casual cocktail party conversation. And if you don't actually engage in casual cocktail

---

[1] It's not an *acronym* according to my editor who knows shit.

[2] Non-letter characters used to mask dirty or profane words are called *maledicta* by some. Others call them *grawlix*, though I found a reference that indicates that *grawlix* is only a swirly character. You be the judge.

party conversation, perhaps because you are 14 years old and have already sold your first mobile crypto AI media web technology company that has some nonsense word as its company name like *Zizzout* or *Deelonic* or something, then maybe you can use this term in a derogatory fashion when discussing old people, as in "He's such an EBITDA, I'll bet he doesn't have his *Deelonic* account geo-back-linked to his *Zizzout* account."

Some More Preface

This book isn't very long. By the time you are finished reading the entire book, your plane should have landed in San Francisco, if you are on a plane to San Francisco from, say, Boston. I wrote some of this book in 1996 and put most of it on a website called Steve's Financial Modeling Tutorial, which is no longer around. You can find other sites that are sad copies of it and all the information here is on the web, of course, in various, shitty forms, but the web is now so impossible to navigate, reading this book is the smartest thing you have done in the last ten seconds. You could get all this information for free from the web[3], but you didn't—otherwise you wouldn't be reading this, et cetera.

Recently (as of today, which is not when you are reading this, so take it on faith that when I wrote this sentence, it was recently[4]), because of a job loss and insomnia, I decided to finish this book. I'm not sure if I'll make any money, but I sure as shit know how to figure out if it makes any money. (That's a joke.)

---

[3] Something that really pissed me off is MS Word capitalizing *Web*, as if it's some important place like Charley's Steakhouse or The B-Cup Lounge in Pattaya, Thailand. Fuck that. It's *web*, lowercase. I will die on this hill.

[4] So, it's no longer recently since this is the second edition; it's like two decades later and I've seen some shit.

I assume in this book that you are building a **financial model**—a series of financial statements in a spreadsheet program to reflect or predict the financial state of a business— or that you wish to understand how to read financial statements. If you are not creating a financial model, you will still be able to understand and learn from this book because it is written in English and you speak English.[5]

This book will not help you invest better. It will not help you manage your money or make you rich. You may even end up investing in some company or starting a business because you understand financial statements but lose lots of money, and that's sometimes what happens. But this book will teach you to understand the basic components of financial statements and why they are important and how to model a small enterprise or a big enterprise using a spreadsheet.

I created Steve's Financial Modeling Tutorial in the late 1990s to help folks like me understand how to make a financial model. I called it *Steve's Financial Modeling Tutorial* because I'm a narcissist. I was working for a boutique investment firm that focused on a single asset class—in our case, global forestry products—until 1998, so it was sometime before that. "Boutique

---

[5] It's theoretically possible that this book will be translated into French or Klingon or something and then this thought will devolve into some kind of recursive/*Inception* mind-fuck.

investment firm" typically means a firm owned by a single individual, usually someone with a serious personality disorder. Other former employees who are more litigiously prone than I am can tell you if that was true. That firm isn't around anymore. Go figure.

I basically forgot about the website for a long time. And during that time, I would get occasional emails from folks thanking me for helping them understand basic finance. For example, I got this one many, many years ago:

> Name: D. B.
>
> Greatly appreciate your financial modeling tutorial, especially the tone and prose! I do multivariate modeling. You make sense everywhere.

Seriously, a guy who does "multivariate modeling" says that I make sense. Go figure. (I say "go figure" a lot because it sounds dryly ironic and makes me sound smart.)

For many years Steve's Financial Modeling Tutorial was the first result on Google for *financial modeling.*

Since I'm actually kind of lazy, I never did anything cool with Steve's Financial Modeling Tutorial like make a message board, build a financial/social networking site, build interactive modeling tools, or make any money from it. Nothing. I did absolutely nothing. Seriously. I totally squandered my opportunity to build what could have been the most important financial education site in the world, but instead I got married and got divorced and got cancer and other shit. The site is dead now. [cue old car horn failure sound].

Then in 2002 I dramatically updated the website. Or so I said to site visitors. But I can't remember what I actually did at that time. I certainly didn't do anything like turn the website into a business so I could pay my bills or make it more usable or anything that an actual site visitor would care about. I probably didn't do anything at all; I just said I did. Like when food conglomerates change the packaging on their *Fatty Fatsticks* fried fat sticks and call them *"New! Better-Tasting Fatty Fatsticks"* fried fat sticks and everyone really knows it's the same *Fatty Fatsticks* from before but we buy them anyway because they are made of fat and salt and that's always a compelling food combination.

I ignored the site (again) for many years while I slaved away on my start-up, a property listing service for rural property. (I have a degree in forestry.) When I sold LandAndFarm.com in July 2008, the financial modeling tutorial site went off-line because I'm too stupid to realize when I've got something that people want.

Because of impending poverty, college tuition for my kids,

ex-wife payments,[6] the desire for fame, and the fact that a guy who wants to know finance broke into my house and is pointing a gun at my head (please notify the authorities), I'm finishing this mother cunt fucking goddamn fuck-ass[7] book.

You can find the financial models referenced in this book and other examples and links to some good porn and shit on my website. Most importantly, the site has the *Habitable Exoplanet Visualizer* (I'm not kidding), which has absolutely nothing to do with financial modeling because if you get good at financial modeling you actually get to do shit you enjoy, like figure out when nearby stellar systems first received episodes of *Knocked Up and Totin*[8], the definitive porn series about pregnant women who carry guns.

I created the original tutorial website and started this book to help some of my friends who had finance questions but couldn't find simple answers anywhere. I had to teach myself all this stuff and it was a pain, so I always thought it would be good to pass on some of this information to others. It's been 20 fucking years since I wrote that first financial modeling tutorial,

---

[6] Who knew that ex-wives are actually more expensive than wives? Not me. How do you make $1 million? Start with $2 million and get divorced.

[7] Foul language my editor said I should delete.

[8] So, when I was in my twenties, Times Square still had those magazine kiosks with dozens of hard-core porn magazines on binder clips strung up across the facade. I am not kidding when I tell you there was one called *Knocked Up and Totin'* with a picture of a mostly nude pregnant hottie wielding two revolvers. I really wish I had bought it.

so I'm pretty sure all these questions are answered elsewhere by now, but fuck it, I'm finishing this book.

I'm not an accountant and I've got other personality flaws, and everything in this book is written for someone like me, except for crap like the copyright notice that's written by and for clever, cruel lawyers.

All errors are mine. If you rely solely on this book for financial decision making, wow, you deserve whatever chaos ensues.

Here are the rules of finance:

Rule 1: Do not prepare food on this book.

Rule 2: Preparing financial statements and making financial models is an art. It is possible, even fun, to make financial statements say whatever you want. Bankrupt companies can look healthy. Healthy companies can look bankrupt. You can make a bad business plan have great numbers and a great business plan have bad numbers. There's a bunch of examples of this at the end of the book.

Millions of dollars are invested in crappy ideas with great numbers because investors know as little about financial models as anyone else. Creative accounting is the norm, not the exception.

When you are writing a book, if you are a self-indulgent turd[9] like me, you imagine what reviewers will say. They might say something like the following:

> "Steve's book is a rollicking jaunt through the history of finance, filled with useful knowledge. A wonderful tome to add to your home finance collection."

This book is not that book. This book is this book:

> "A narcissistic regurgitation of bad things done to the author by others, with teasing knowledge about finance occasionally interspersed. It's kind of like *Psycho* meets 'that econ class that nearly caused your death freshman year.' Read it and you might learn a bit about finance or you might just be offended. Frankly, when I finally put it down, I felt dirty and used."

---

[9] Microsoft Word says "turd" is misspelt. It also says "misspelt" is misspelt. What is goodspeak[1a] for "turd"?

[1a] Reference to George Orwell's *1984*. BTW, this is the first use of a footnote within a footnote in a book published in the United States (unconfirmed claim). I had to use all the force of my computer might to get my publishing program to make it work.

Who Should Read This Book?

Anyone who is interested in finance will be helped by reading this book, but it is aimed at those with little or no experience or training in finance and at people who compulsively buy books.

Appropriate readers include

- students,
- entrepreneurs,
- small-business owners,
- journalists, and
- people trapped at home during violent storms.
    - (Just FYI, today, honest truth, it is winter in New England and I am trapped in my home during a violent storm.)

What Is Financial Modeling?

Companies generate numbers like cows generate methane. There are zillions of financial numbers that are generated by companies every day and every minute and every second. And it's all good. Because without the numbers, how would companies know when to lay people off or raise prices? There are lots of numbers that companies calculate, such as

- last week's sales in the Tulsa store;
- the amount of money in the company bank account;
- total inventory of anal lube;
- the salary of Angelika, the hot secretary of the guy who does something in legal;
- how much was stolen by the CFO;
- et cetera.

Every single one of these numbers goes into or comes from one or more of the three basic financial statements: the **income statement**, the **cash flow statement**, and the **balance sheet**. Once you learn the basics of financial modeling, you will be able to think of everything a company does as affecting the income statement, the cash flow statement, or the balance sheet, or any combination thereof, therefore, and thereto.

It is important to realize that financial modeling isn't accounting. It is a means for managers and entrepreneurs (and members of the conspiracy of the *Knights Templar* and the *partisan front*) to guess what the future will hold.[10] And I am not an accountant. And you are not an accountant (unless you are). We are not accountants.[11]

My tone in this book varies from deadly serious to ridiculously sarcastic. Sometimes I am liberal with grammar rules. I use foul language and cuss a lot.[12] I make fun of people who cannot defend themselves. I make fun of myself as well. I hope it is easy to read, even fun to read. I may include some tidbits on other topics and the occasional anecdote, but you can be sure that I actually like talking about this stuff. Well, I used to like talking about this. Now, not so sure.

Definition:

Financial Modeling: The process of either analyzing or making a set of predictive financial statements.

---

[10] Always in motion is the future. —Yoda

[11] Q: Are We Not Men? A: We Are Devo!

[12] Yes, I said "cuss." Because I grew up in Maryland and that's what we called a "curse." And when I went to college in New England, other kids made fun of me for saying "y'all" and "cuss" and I stopped using those bits of southern lingo to avoid the daily taunting. Now that I'm publishing my own book, I can say "cuss" and those kids who made fun of me can go suck eggs and cuss at the moon.

Who Am I?

I am Moloch, who comes from the Darkness to smite the unbelievers! Bow your heads, ugly flesh tubes![13]

I'm also Steven Saltman, a ne'er-do-well[14] dot-commer who once had a high-flying job as an investment professional and then founded LandAndFarm.com, a website. In July 2008 I sold LandAndFarm.com to Loopnet. I used my mastery of financial modeling to make the sale happen. Well, not really, but it's helpful to be able to talk to your potential buyer about cash flow[15] without having to call someone with an MBA for help.

Here are more fun facts about Steve:

I've built hundreds of financial models, some of which actually predicted financial performance. I have found my own skills in financial modeling invaluable when planning for my business. For example, it's always helpful to know exactly how far behind on your mortgage you will be on your wife's birthday.

---

[13] This was in the first edition. I have no idea why I thought this was funny. I was gonna delete it, but life is short.

[14] "Ne'er-do-well"—noun. A self-indulgent person who spends time avoiding work or other useful activity: bum, drone, good-for-nothing, idler, lay-about, loafer, no-good, slugabed, sluggard, wastrel, do-little, do-nothing, lazybones, slug, slouch.

[15] There is a difference of opinion about whether "cashflow" is one word or two words. I'm using one word here. I used two words in other places. Nobody can stop me.

I'm now divorced and don't have to worry about my wife's birthday anymore, but the point is still valid.

I personally ran a whole mess of other websites, and except for those that were built or designed by my friends and colleagues, these sites are mostly failures that don't work or don't provide any value to anyone. *Exempli gratia*, I once had a site called *The International Synonyms for Vomit List*. This site was extremely popular for about six months in the mid-1990s. Naturally I did not have a backup of it and it is now long gone, not even visible on the Web archive. It was hosted on AOL.

I'm a cancer survivor[16] and I've had malaria and a heart attack and a *fundoplication*[17] and I don't donate during blood drives except to suicidal people and my sworn enemies, who luckily are not numerous or important enough to mention here.

I've run a half dozen marathons, none of them very fast.

I can tie a one-handed bowline knot, which is useful if you are at the bottom of a well or cliff and the only way to get up is to have someone throw you a line and one of your arms is broken. However, I can tie a one-handed bowline knot only with my right hand, so if my left arm is broken, I'm in good shape, but if my right arm is broken, I'm fucked like the rest of the "no

---

[16] I wrote a book about that called *Diagnosis + 6 Days*. You can buy 4,000 copies on Amazon today if you want.

[17] I cannot get life insurance, natch.

one-handed bowline knowledge" proletariat masses.[18]

I don't like pizza.

All of my businesses have been sold or shut down. I am writing science fiction and sometime around the publication of this book, my first science fiction novel, *Adventures in Radio Astronomy*, should be published.

I am trapped in my house by aliens wielding colonoscopy equipment. Please call the police.

---

[18] There are videos of folks tying one-handed bowline knots on the interwebs.

A Note on Spreadsheets

Generally, when trying to estimate the profitability of an activity or an enterprise, you need to add and/or subtract a bunch of numbers. These numbers represent the revenue or costs of the business **at a single point in time** or **over periods of time**, or they represent the value of **something the company owns or owes**. The best way to do this nowadays is with a spreadsheet program. There are many spreadsheet programs out there and I'm hardly an expert on all of them, though I've used a few.

I used to use Microsoft Excel for all my financial modeling. It was the best. Before Excel there was Lotus, and before that there was VisiCalc,[19] but Excel beat them all. When I started in finance, Excel was already the leader. And every year it got better. It was easy. You could customize it. It had all the tools at your fingertips. This was in the 1990s.

---

[19] I've met Dan Bricklin, inventor of VisiCalc. To a financial geek, that's like how meeting the first upright primate would be to an evolutionary biologist.

Excel 2003 and the Bad Odor

Then came Excel 2003. It was so bad that I can only compare it to the memory of an odor I smelled in Paraguay in 1987 when I had just finished college and my friend Alex and I hopped on a flight to Asunción and a week later we found ourselves in the middle of dozens of stalls of meat sellers in the public market. For decades, perhaps centuries, the blood and sinew and offal from the work of the butchers of the Asunción public meat market had fallen and been stomped into the market's dirt floor. Now that layer of biological refuse was slowly rotting in the jungle-like humidity. The odor was truly magnificent, like the pain of being punched squarely in the nose. It was so bad, I wish I could have captured it on smell-o-film so I could share it with you. It was an epic smell. And I remember reading in the international press years later that the shopkeepers in the Asunción market had actually rioted to get the government to help clean up the piles of rotting garbage so that the market could function better.[20] Excel 2003 was that bad.

In the decades since, Excel versions have improved again, and Google Sheets and various other spreadsheets all work well

---

[20] I cannot find a reference to that article on the Web, so maybe I imagined it.

enough to do financial modeling.

Financial modeling doesn't require great computing power or amazing complexity. A spreadsheet is the best way to do it. And that spreadsheet program should be able to

- calculate addition, subtraction, multiplication, and division;
- create absolute and relative references;
- change formatting across several different worksheets;
- be able to do a simple "if...then" statement within a cell; and
- find the source references for cells, usually called the "trace" function in spreadsheet applications.

Use whatever works for you.

Tim Morton and the Numbers

I once worked with a guy named Tim Morton[21] who was our chief financial officer. I always thought of EBITDA as Earnings Before Interest, Taxes, Depreciation, and Tim Mortonization, even though the acronym doesn't match those words. When I was really bored during our investment committee meetings, which was often, especially when our founder would go on and on about his great days on Wall Street, I would come up with new definitions of the acronym:

- Earnings Before Interest, Taxes, Depreciation, and Amalgamation
- Eggs Before Intestines, Tortellini, and Defecation
- Eek, Betty, I Touched Denise's Ass
- Elephant Balls ID'd: Totally Don't Ask

This made me chuckle during investment committee

---

[21] Not his real name. Seriously. It's not. Because if it were his real name and he were offended by being called chief financial officer (as would any sane person), then he could sue me for defamation or slander or libel. (I still don't really know the difference between those three.) And even though there is a legal axiom that the truth is a defense, I really don't want to get into a legal pissing match with some guy whose name isn't Tim Morton.

meetings, and since I sometimes chuckled without engaging my Internal-Only Chuckle Control System, or IOCCS, my chuckle would then be heard by the rest of the investment committee, usually followed by an awkward moment of silence that lasted until I realized everyone was either staring at me or, like the administrative staff and whoever else was in the room, nervously glancing at their laps. Folks would think I was not paying attention or was having a "Steve moment" because I was chuckling to myself, when in fact, I was paying perfect attention. Otherwise, I wouldn't know that we were going over EBITDA, aka *The Numbers*.

And when I say *The Numbers*, I mean the financial numbers. The profit and loss. The P&L. The Bottom Line. Earnings. Net income, et cetera. EBITDA is a representation of how much money the business made, is making, or is going to make. This is the basic question of business. And calculating how much money the business is making is itself a business, one conducted by consultants, accountants, financiers, and, in reality, anyone in business.

One could even argue, since arguing is kind of fun, that anyone who handles money in any way, shape, or form is calculating earnings. So when your kids are spending their lunch money, they may be thinking, "Mom gave me $4. Lunch costs $3.56; therefore, I'll have 44 cents left to hide in my run-away-from-home stash." And that calculation—what your kid got ($4) and what your kid spent ($3.56)—is a calculation of profit or earnings or net something.

The Heisenberg Uncertainty Principle says that the more you try to examine something, the less accurate your examination will be. Calculating profit can be equally elusive. You can take a simple business, like making paper (inputs: trees, water, power; output: paper), and by the time you are finished examining every aspect of the business, you have proved only that you have no idea whether the company is making money.[22]

---

[22] This has more to do with the incredibly high cost of paper-making machines than anything else.

Financial Jargon

I believe that everyone should know how to read financial statements. And by that, I mean "everyone should know how to read financial statements." I imply no irony in that statement. Certainly, entrepreneurs should know the basics of finance. So should housewives and teachers and everyone, even people you don't like. And you don't need to get an MBA or become an accountant to know this stuff. Most people can use a calculator and do pretty complex math without being mathematicians, and many people can put on a bandage without being a doctor, so why shouldn't everyone know how to read financial statements? Or even better, everyone should be able to create a set of financial statements for their business or their house or their life.

If you have a business and don't know if it is making money, how will you know if you can afford Christmas presents? I know that sounds like a vicious and brutal attack on the spirit of giving, but it is not an unreasonable question to ask. Also, how will you eat your cake if you don't eat your pudding?

I worked in Russia in 1992 (Jesus fucking *Christ, I'm old*) for a group of investors who wanted to invest in newly privatizing

Russian sawmills (my degree is in forestry[23]—did I say that already?), and one morning, like many mornings, I spent several hours describing to a group of Russian senior managers at a sawmill near Petrozavodsk[24] the reasons why my employers wanted to invest in the Russian forestry products industry. After we had talked for two hours through a translator and after a shot of pre-breakfast vodka, I was asked by a gray-suited, red-faced Russian bureaucrat, "Что же это такое, выгода?" meaning, "What is this thing called profit?"[25]

Where was I to begin with an answer? Clearly, the moment called for more vodka and a bowl of borscht. Because figuring out profit isn't as easy it looks.

But first a note on *jargon*, because you need to understand that financial jargon is the chasm that separates the financially literate few from folks like us (well, really *you*, since I know this stuff, but I didn't always know it, so I can sympathize).

I think sometimes jargon is actually used to maintain

---

[23] My degree is actually an MEM—Master of Environmental Management, which is what Duke University invented when *forestry* became *persona non grata* at the beginning of the *green* movement.

[24] Sister city of Duluth, Minnesota. To read an amazing tale about the region, get the book *They Took My Father* by Mayme Sevander, which is about a family that emigrated to the Republic of Karelia in the Soviet Union from Wisconsin in 1934—that's right, they left the USA and went to Russia.

[25] He might not have said exactly that since I don't have some kind of recorder in my brain and it was through a translator after several shots of vodka.

knowledge in the hands of the few. And this is where I will mention my own conspiracy theory that the hidden descendants of the *Knights Templar* create financial jargon to maintain their secret control on the global banking system from their secret lair... Or something. Somewhere on the internet someone believes this.

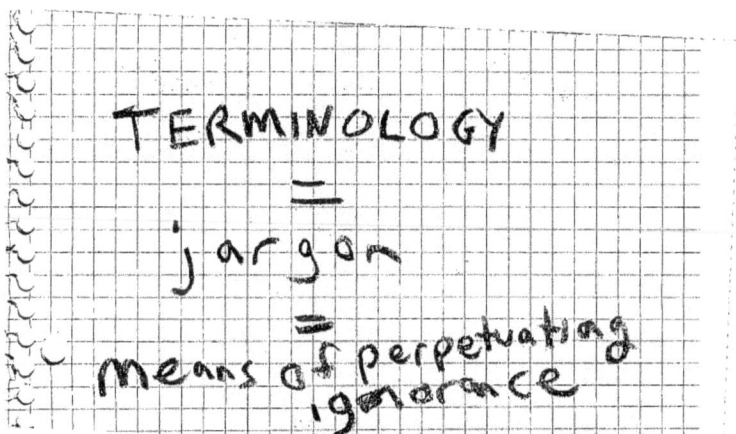

TERMINOLOGY
=
jargon
=
means of perpetuating ignorance

So ideally this little book is helping to break down that jargon barrier and will allow you to ascend into the realm of the blessed few who speak the speak and talk the talk.

In the financial press I've seen a lot of phrases for a company's various types of earnings or profit:

Finance Phrase Builder[26]

Choose One Word	Choose One Word	Build Financial Jargon
net	revenue	net revenue
gross	income	net income
marginal	earnings	net earnings
	profit	net profit
	margin	net margin
		gross revenue
		gross income
		gross earnings
		et al

And, of course, there are more combinations such as "net profit margin" and "gross profit margin" and the unfathomable EBITDA.

Honestly, every single phrase in the third column could be used in a corporate press release describing how much money was made and very few people would criticize or comment on the terminology.

---

[26] This table is loosely based on the Web Economy Bullshit Generator once, and perhaps still, at Dack.com.

I'm going to get hate mail from business school professors and accountants telling me that there are very specific definitions for each of these word combinations. But I say bullshit. Most folks didn't go to business school, so such academic definitions are useless, and I don't know the definitions and I'm writing this book. And furthermore, I spent years in finance talking to investors and CEOs and I spent a shitload of time on the internet researching some of this crap to make sure I didn't publish anything that was completely incorrect (partial incorrectness, however…), and all I found were a lot of websites filled with pay-per-click advertising and crappy definitions that didn't help me and lots and lots of porn.

And this isn't to say that it doesn't matter if you use the right terminology; if you can, you should. But for most people this jargon adds a consistent barrier to grasping finance unless they have had specific training. I've read a lot of articles in the Financial Times and the Wall Street Journal, and I cannot claim to know the difference between net profit and gross profit when they're used to describe a random company. And this type of obfuscatory[27] language simply confuses everyone.

On top of all that, even if we had a single definitive phrase for the various ways to calculate profit, most people still don't

---

[27] Today's goal: Use "obfuscatory" in a sentence.

understand the way things like depreciation or other non-cash costs are accounted for in a company's financial statements, so the terminology is meaningless, and a company could say they earned $1 billion in gross profit revenue and they may as well have spent $1 billion on ear wax replacement therapy for the CEO's mistress/chief marketing officer and only a few analysts on Wall Street would be able to figure it out.

So, I'll try to stick to consistent terminology (and I'll fail) and more importantly explain how I calculated the numbers in this book.

Financial statements, particularly audited financial statements, are one of the only ways an investor or a government agency can determine the health of a company.

Very early in my career I was unemployed and needed a job quick. I was living in Washington, DC in my mom's basement (yes, I am a stereotype). I took a job with the Government National Mortgage Association, also known as Ginnie Mae. You may have heard of Fannie Mae, its sister organization, or Freddie Mac, its cousin.

Ginnie Mae[28] helped small banks by guaranteeing mortgage-

---

[28] Also, interesting story: I applied for that job before email and cell phones, I had no choice but to literally sit by the phone hoping someone would call back. After getting no response for a few days, I wrote the head of the division a thank-you for considering me but not offering me (cont...) the job. I got a phone call a day or so later from him, apologizing. He thought I had already started, but, in a weird administrative blooper, nobody had

backed securities. Basically, banks would lend money to homeowners. The banks could then sell the mortgages, guaranteed by Ginnie Mae. After selling the mortgages, the banks could lend again. This increased the availability of mortgages. All good, right? A decade or two after I worked at Ginnie Mae, Fannie Mae would get into this business big-time and encourage so much lending, we'd get the 2008 financial crisis.

But this was way before that. And my job was to review the financial statements of banks that were in the Ginnie Mae ecosystem and try to find some red flags to indicate which banks were about to go belly up and their portfolio of mortgages would end up being covered by the taxpayers.

When I showed up at Ginnie Mae, I knew nothing about banking or finance. I'd never read a financial statement in my life. I didn't know what a balance sheet was. My uncle Marty, one of the smartest people I've known, told me not to underestimate the work, which I had complained seemed very dull. "Most people can't read a financial statement," he said.

I was given access to a room full of file cabinets containing every annual report of every bank that lent money under the Ginnie Mae programs. I was told simply, "Find out something

---

finalized my hiring. I started a day later.

about the worst banks." Ginnie Mae wanted to identify problem banks early.

I started reading financial statements. Since this was before the internet, I had to go to the public library to get some books on finance just so I could understand some of the terms, like *liabilities* and *retained earnings*.

After reading hundreds of audited financial statements of banks and building a spreadsheet of data related to those banks, such as current ratios, debt ratios, and others, my conclusion was clear: the biggest red flag for Ginnie Mae was late or missing audited financial statements.

That's right—the biggest indicator that a bank was in trouble was not in the financial statements themselves, but was clearly indicated if the bank sent in their required, audited financial statements late or didn't send them at all.

About two weeks after I submitted my report, I was seconded to the private contractor that Ginnie Mae hired to manage the collateralized mortgage program. This contractor was nearby in much nicer offices.

On the second day there, during a staff meeting, the head honcho of that program got up and described to the entire team how Ginnie Mae had found a red flag for bad banks. I braced myself for being singled out as the discoverer of this great news.

But then he announced with great disdain that missing

audited financials were the biggest red flag. He laughed, dismissing the report as useless and irrelevant. Everyone in the room laughed with him, and that was the end of the discussion. I shrank into the back, not understanding why my findings were being dismissed.

I think, in retrospect, the fact that no great mathematical correlation or analysis, but rather simple administrative evidence, was the easiest way to spot problem banks made the contractors' work less important.

If bad banks could simply be flagged when they missed a filing deadline, why would a contractor need a dozen financial analysts poring over financial statements?

I left and went to grad school. And a decade or so later came *The Big Short.*[29]

---

[29] *The Big Short: Inside the Doomsday Machine* is a nonfiction book by Michael Lewis about the buildup of the United States housing bubble during the 2000s.

The Difficulty of Calculating Profit

Let's just say for a moment that the world is a very simple place. And in this simple place, which we'll call Boston, Massachusetts [cue laughter], you sell hot dogs at a place called Fenway Park from a blue cooler that you carry around the bleachers during baseball games. You hoist the cooler onto your shoulder every time there's a game. Your shoulder hurts, but you love baseball. The lifestyle is killing you since your entire diet consists of *Tylenol*, *Advil*, and unsold inventory, but you love baseball. In this simple place, the people are also very simple and they are willing to pay you $10 for a hot dog. Yes, 10 fucking dollars.

Outrageous! you say. Choose a more realistic example, you say.

No! I say. I will create an extremely unlikely scenario so that we can focus only on the numbers and not on the fabricated, unlikely, preposterous situation that could never exist such as anyone paying $10 for a compressed, salty, baked amalgam of pureed beef (we hope) parts, which are surprisingly tasty just like *Fatty Fatsticks* brand fat sticks (a fictional product invented by my son).

Anyway, you sell a hot dog for $10. What's your profit?

Ha! Gotcha. You are quick if you figured out that your profit is unknown. To calculate profit we need to know how much you paid for the hot dog. The profit is allegedly, supposedly, and possibly the amount you paid for the hot dog—your cost— minus the amount you received—your revenue.

If you paid $1 for the hot dog and you sold it for $10, you made $9 profit. Pretty simple.

But if the owners of Fenway Park, who shall remain nameless because I didn't Google the answer, say you have to wear an officially licensed Fenway Park branded baseball jersey that cost them $2.52 from a Malaysian sweatshop but that you have to purchase from them for $40 as part of the business agreement to sell hot dogs within Fenway Park, did you make a profit? The answer isn't so clear. You made money on the hot dog, true. But your business has less money than when it started, right? So what's your profit? Well, the profit on the hot dog was $9, but you've spent $40 on the jersey.

Revenue

hot dog $10

Expenses

hot dog $1

jersey $40

Profit

WTF? $9?

          $39?

          $0?

The answer depends on how you account for the jersey. And if you say you know the answer, you are a lying son of a bitch.[30] This example is basically where finance devolves from a simple mathematical subtraction exercise into a complex accounting exercise that requires three financial statements.

---

[30] Two squirrels are in a tree arguing. One says, "This is a beech." The other says, "This is a birch." They call over the woodpecker to resolve their dispute. He pecks the tree and says, "This ain't no son of a beech and this ain't no son of a birch. This is the best piece of ash I ever stuck my pecker in."

Revenue Is the Top Line

I will point out that I put revenue as the first line of the example above. This is standard operating procedure in finance, and that is why revenue is called the *top line*. Profit is last, and that is why folks talk about the *bottom line*. If you didn't know that, you do now.

Definition—**revenue**

- Anything that comes in from the sale of a good or service. It is the mathematical product (meaning multiplication) of price and quantity. If I have 10 hot dogs and sell them for $10 each, then my revenue is $100.

- Revenue = price × quantity

This little definition is something you'd learn in an economics class. And you'll find that some of the stuff we talk about in this book is from economics. Some more of the information in this book is from accounting and some is from finance, and some is from your junior high school lunchroom.

It's no wonder most folks never learnt[31] how to read a financial statement—you need to distill a wide range of staggeringly boring information from several stupidly uninteresting academic disciplines to get to the basics of finance.

Profit is a complex thing. Take the following scenarios: (Don't worry about not understanding some of the jargon. By the time you land in San Francisco, you'll understand.)

Scenario 1—temporally dislocated selling

I buy a hot dog for $1. I fail to sell it that day and head home. On the way home I'm "accidentally" run over by an MBTA bus and my brains are splattered all over Yawkey Way. I'm very dead. My blue cooler containing the hot dog disappears.

A thousand years later that blue cooler is discovered by my descendants behind a stack of old porn magazines in the basement of my old house, which amazingly had never been cleaned—the apple doesn't fall far from the tree, eh? My entrepreneurial descendants sell the blue cooler on eBay for C€500,000[32] after they discover the last surviving Fenway Park hot dog. It is a very valuable hot dog; Fenway Park having been torn down once baseball was outsourced to the newly created

---

[31] Bucket list item crossed off: to use "learnt" instead of "learned."
[32] Crypto-euros replaced G-credits after the Martian Wars in 2355.

undersea tax haven of *The Republic of Smittoobo*.

Quote from Sotheby's press release on the sale: "The dried-out Fenway Frank fetched a good price despite the fact that it looks like a mummified corpse of a miniature Dachshund."

Was the transaction profitable for me?

Answer: No. I am dead.

Scenario 2—immediate profit calculations

What if I buy a hot dog for $1 and calculate my profit five seconds later, before I sell it? Do I have a profit?

Answer: Nope, but I also don't have a loss and I have $1 in hot dog inventory, which would be quite obvious if you looked at your fucking balance sheet.

Scenario 3—accruing the dog

What if I run out of hot dogs and Some Fat Guy in the Stands (acronym: SFGITS, pronounced *sfigits*) gives me $10 and asks me to go get a hot dog from the hot dog kiosk, where they cost $8, and bring the hot dog back to him in the stands, and he adds in a pompous sneer so he can look generous to his buddies at the game, "Keep the change"?[33] Before I get the hot dog, but after he gives me the money, do I have profit?

Answer: Yes, on an accrual basis. I have $10 in revenue and $8 in accrued expenses. That's $2 profit. On a theft basis (a different kind of accounting used by only the most discriminating conglomerates) I have made $10. (It's profit only if you keep it, but you better run before SFGITS figures out you aren't returning with his hot dog.) On a cash basis... who the fuck knows?

Scenario 4—ugly dog loss

Five minutes into the bottom of the ninth inning, two outs, nobody on, Red Sox down by seven, I still have one hot dog that I bought for $1. I'm unlikely to sell it since most of the fans have left already. Besides being depressed about the loss, I'm stuck with this fucking cold hot dog, which is turning white as fats congeal on its waxy, polypropylene skin. It has become worthless, except to my neighbor's ugly dog. If I bring the hot dog home, my neighbor will buy the hot dog for 50 cents to feed to his ugly dog. So I bring it to my neighbor, who gives me 50 cents. The dog gets a free hot dog. What's my profit?

---

[33] He must be a [team other than the Red Sox] fan.

Answer: I have a loss of 50 cents. The dog is still ugly.

Scenario 5—friendly profit and loss

I buy a hot dog for $1. My friend Bob is in the stands and says he has no money but will gladly pay me $10 tomorrow for a hot dog now. I agree and give him a hot dog. Did I make any money?

Answer: On a cash basis, I have lost $1. Seriously, has Bob ever kept his fucking word? Assuming everyone else in the world agrees that Bob's word is shit, then I have just given away $1 of hot dog. But, on an accrual basis, I have a profit of $9. I have accounts receivable (A/R in finance lingo[34]) of $10 on my balance sheet.

Scenario 6—Bob again

I see Bob[35] in the stands. Instead of promising me $10 tomorrow, he gives me $1 now and promises me $9 tomorrow. Did I make a profit?

Answer: On a cash basis I am at break even. On an accrual

---

[34] Lingo = jargon. I will pontificate on jargon later in this book.
[35] What do you call an armless and legless man floating in the ocean?

basis, I have a profit of $9 and have accounts receivable on my balance sheet of $9.

Scenario 7—no idea what to call this

I buy 75 hot dogs for $75 total. I sell 1 hot dog for $10. Do I have a profit? Now, this is an interesting question, eh?[36]

I mean, I made a profit on the hot dog I sold, but I have lots of hot dogs left. WTF? I have 1,000 percent margins on the fucking hot dogs, but I'm broke! This. Can. Not. Be. Happening!

Ahahahhahahahggggggggg…

Answer: Whether I have a profit depends on how I want to model my revenue. If I break my time periods into very discrete (small) units, I could show that single hot dog sale during one period and show a profit for that period. And, in reality, as long as the hot dogs in my inventory don't decline in value, I could show a profit over any time period. My cash flow, however, won't look so good. But since I can report just profit to Wall Street, my stock will go up, despite the fact that my hot dog retailing company is fucked like a milf in a frat house.

---

[36] I am not Canadian.

And on it goes...

Calculating profit depends on many factors. It matters how much I paid for the hot dog. It matters when I sell it, for how much, when I am paid, and how I have decided to account for money I have not received. And how I will account for any equipment I need to be in business.

What Is an Accountant?

Why do they exist? Are they rich? Where do their children go to school?

Before we get into financial statements, let me try to give you some insight into the role of an accountant.

When I make financial statements by building a financial model in a spreadsheet program, the statements are only as accurate as I make them—meaning they are full of guesswork and most people will look at them and perhaps not laugh out loud, but will instead roll their eyes and mutter "Why me?" Financial statements you or I produce are not the same as the financial statements in an *annual report*—those are prepared by accountants following complex accounting rules.

Companies need better financial statements than those produced by someone who could have had a life but instead chose to write this book. So, they turn to an accountant—someone who has the credentials and training to charge a lot of money to make financial statements. A financial professional who has gone through an initiation process, which I understand can be seen on the internet if you have SafeSearch turned off, is called a *certified public accountant*, or CPA.[37]

Accountants are common in the wild and are native to Western cultures. And if a CPA is tempted, caught, and appeased by large amounts of cash from a company, he or she may agree to give financial statements the blessing of the CPA (which I hear is done naked) and the financial statements are then called *audited financial statements*.

Audited financial statements are what public companies are required to show shareholders. And many private investors and lenders require that level of financial responsibility from companies they invest in and lend to.

Only a CPA can produce audited financial statements. Audited financial statements are created following strict rules so that the statements of the local dry cleaner are generally produced with the same methodology as those produced for Amazon.com, Inc. The rules an accountant follows to create audited financial statements are called "Generally Accepted Accounting Principles," or GAAP.[38]

I do not produce *audited* financial statements and do not have the training to do so. If you are not an accountant, then

---

[37] Actually, It's a bunch of coursework and tests.

[38] All this shit about GAAP refers to the USA. Don't call me from France in a panic and say, *"Mon dieu,* asshole, I just got fired from my job with BancFranc because your info is all *muy mal."* I'm sure there's a French equivalent of GAAP, probably called PAAG, but I don't know shit about it.

you cannot produce *audited* financial statements either. But I can produce, as can anyone, financial statements that are accurate given whatever information is available—no CPA needed. But any financial statements produced by someone who isn't an accountant are worth about as much as yesterday's news, unless you are a hedge fund analyst, in which case your analyses are probably worth more than Tibet.

A Note on GAAP

GAAP are the rules that accountants (are supposed to) follow when they perform audits and make financial statements. Of course, since accounting is necromancy, GAAP is the Necronomicon.[39] Like a religious tome, GAAP is simply interpreted by accountants to fit their needs, though some rules are pretty hard and fast. You don't need to follow GAAP when creating a financial model in a spreadsheet program. In fact, **you can't follow GAAP when creating a financial model** because you can't collect enough information and your model would be too complex and error filled at the same time, and it would not be a useful predictor of financial performance. But you could try if you like self-flagellation.

Going one step further into the rabbit hole… FASAB stands for the Financial Accounting Standards Advisory Board. This is the ~~coven~~ professional organization that sets all those accounting rules. Though in reality they don't even do that; they let the accountants set the rules through an organization called the American Institute of Certified Public Accountants, or

---

[39] *Necronomicon* is a book that never existed. It is mentioned in short stories by H. P. Lovecraft. Since Lovecraft's death many people have published various occult-genre books under that title.

AICPA. You really don't need to know any of this shit, unless you want to watch the FASAB initiation ceremony, which I hear includes raw shellfish and underinflated volleyballs.

The FASAB is a US government body. Other countries probably have equally ponderous and impenetrable agencies to help confuse investors and maintain the status quo.

Here's what FASAB has to say about GAAP:

The term "generally accepted accounting principles" has a specific meaning for accountants and auditors. **The AICPA Code of Professional conduct prohibits members from expressing an opinion or stating affirmatively that financial statements or other financial data "present fairly... in conformity with generally accepted accounting principles," if such information contains any departures from accounting principles promulgated by a body designated by the AICPA Council to establish such principles.**[40]

I want to comment on the second sentence, which I have

---

[40] *FASAB Handbook*, Version 19 (06/20), page 5.

highlighted. It is my belief that this sentence was written by a drunkard who fell into a vat of cough syrup. Cthulu[41] himself would not be able to write worse English if he even spoke English, though it is possible that he wrote that sentence. If you can rewrite that sentence better, do it. Holy Toledo, the douche who wrote that sentence should be [censored] by a homophobic presidential candidate using a spatula. Incomprehensible gibberish.

GAAP is important when looking at a company's financial statements because a company can muck around with its financial reporting fairly significantly. Without rules like GAAP a company could basically say they were profitable when they were not. Of course, no company would ever do such a thing. Ever. Really never ever.

GAAP tries to make everything apples-to-apples between companies. It fails, but that's the real world for you.

Moving on…

---

[41] Cthulhu is a monster created by horror author H. P. Lovecraft in 1926.

The Most Important Finance Graphic Ever

There are three basic financial statements:

- **Balance Sheet**—everything you own and owe.

- **Income Statement**—how much revenue you received and costs you incurred, whether in cash or as empty promises made during tear-filled nights or some other form.

- **Cash Flow Statement**—what came in, what went out.

Whether you are reading financial statements or building financial models, you should understand that you need all three of the above financial statements to understand a company. Most people know how to model only income. For example, "I will make vibrators in the shape of famous dictators[42] for $5.50 each and sell them for $19.95 each." This is only the income and

---

[42] Brand: Dickvators™. BTW, the Putin is sold out. The Trump is orange and always 50% off.

costs, not the whole story.

Some folks understand how to build a balance sheet by adding up all their assets and debts. For example, "I have 12 baggies of coke and 15 opioid tablets, and I owe Bubsy $1,000." But again, this isn't the whole picture.

<u>Balance Sheet</u>

Coke and tabs:	$1500
Owed to Bubsy:	$1000
Net Assets:	$500

And this is one of the biggest problems with EBITDA. On the face of it, EBITDA is a calculation of profit. But really it is an estimate of cash flow. And cash flow is not the same as earnings or profit, or...or...something. Get it?

Two of the financial statements measure the movement of money over time. These are the **income statement** and the **cash flow statement**.

The **balance sheet** is a snapshot of the financial position of a company at a specific moment in time. This is an important point that needs to be remembered. If you have memory problems like I do, then you might want to consider tattooing this on the inside of your eyelids.

The time periods do not need to be years. You can calculate

income and cash flow over any period of time. Likewise the balance sheet doesn't need to be calculated yearly; it can be calculated for any moment in time. And it doesn't even need to be calculated at regular intervals. You can calculate a balance sheet every five minutes if you have some weird sexual need to do so.

Really fucking important graphic…Take a moment from your busy schedule to actually think about this (yea, it looks like two boobs, but for a few seconds of your life, consider that it could look like two finance boobs):

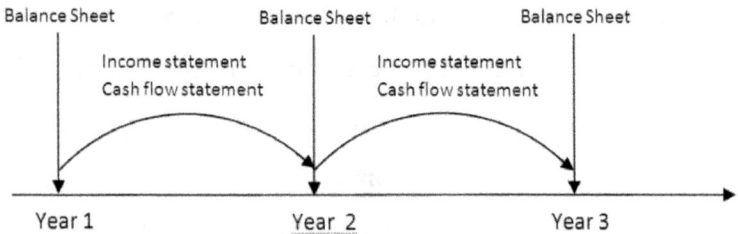

The graph above is the most important finance graphic you will ever see. I have another version I actually drew with crayon, but it sucked, so I made this using MS Word, then did a screenshot, pasted it into MS Paint, and cropped it, and then pasted it back into my word processing software. Pretty good, eh?

Honestly, everything I know about reading financial statements started with this chart. I don't know where I saw it first, maybe in *Penthouse Letters* or the *Bible* or something. Remember this graphic well, even though I will repeat it often.[43] It is more important than your dog-eared copy of *The Joy of Sex* that you keep at the bottom of your night table drawer. It is more important than your *Gmail* password. It is more important than your wedding vows. I will put it on the inside of my coffin, along with instructions on how to defrost me.

Here's the takeaway from that graphic: the balance sheet measures a moment in time, an instant, a *Kodak Moment*, a *Polaroid*, whereas the income statement and cash flow statement measure the movement of money and the promises of money between two points in time.

Understanding financial modeling and understanding how to read financial statements requires understanding how the three financial statements work together. The income statement shows revenue and expenses (whether in cash or otherwise, like your little brother's promise to pay for the weed he stole from your room). The cash flow statement adjusts the revenue statement to back out all the non-cash stuff and the tax-related accounting bullshit to show only real *hard* cash.[44] The balance

---

[43] Actually, I might not repeat it again, so remember it.

[44] Can you believe I used the word "hard" as an adjective to describe cash? Weird. I get a lot of finance spam about "hard money investing," and frankly I think there are some homoerotic implications there that deserve further exploration. Google *hard money* and you'll see what I mean.

sheet shows a moment in time of the company, the result of all the changes from the income and cash flow statements.

This is kind of really awesomely important: All the changes between any two balance sheets can be explained by the income statement and cash flow statements that span the time between them.

The three financial statements are like a mother, a father, and a child. The father is the income statement and makes mad passionate love to the mother, who is the cash flow statement, and nine months later[45] she gives birth to the child, who is the balance sheet. There are probably folks who think that the income statement and the cash flow statement are from a same-sex marriage, but I would counter-argue that perhaps the cash flow statement is more like your addled distant cousin Marvin who likes to eat haggis[46] and the balance sheet is a dead bird your child found in the gutter. Or something.

---

[45] Strangely, that timing is not so far off for producing the balance sheet of a large company.

[46] Scottish sausage honored in a poem by Robert Burns called "Ode to the Haggis." Haggis is traditionally eaten at a Burns supper, which is held around the birthday of Robert Burns. It is the Scottish equivalent of Easter dinner, Thanksgiving dinner, Jewish Seder and a keg party all rolled into one.

The Income Statement

The income statement shows the profit or loss of the company over a specific period of time. At the top of an income statement is the company's revenue, hence the Wall Street jargon *top line* for revenue. (I know I'm repeating myself, I know, I know. It's old age combined with the long-term effects of arguing with anti-vaxxers and toddlers.)

In the middle of an income statement are the expenses of the company, both fixed and variable, and any non-cash expenses (more on this later). At the bottom of an income statement, expenses are subtracted from revenues and you get a profit figure, hence the Wall Street jargon *bottom line* for profit.

The income statement has three parts:

- Revenue (amounts you get from selling goods or services, aka income. See? Two words: Revenue and income that means the same thing, just jargon.)
- Expenses (including non-cash charges such as depreciation, depletion, or amortization[47])
- Profit (revenue minus expenses, aka margin aka net income aka earnings aka many other terms)

---

[47] Tim Mortonization

To answer our question about EBITDA, we want to understand the income statement, because that's where we calculate earnings (the "E").

Here's an income statement I made to model a lemonade stand:

	Month 1	Month 2	Month 3
a. Cups sold, 5%	100	105	110
b. Price @.90	0.90	0.90	0.90
c. Revenue	90.00	94.50	99.00
d. COGS, lemons @.76	76.00	79.80	83.60
e. SGA—signs	2.00	2.00	2.00
f. Earnings	12.00	14.70	15.40

This is a very basic income statement. Let's note a few things. Each line is explained below.

a.   I put the quantity of cups sold on the first line. In a "real" income statement you probably wouldn't put the physical quantity of product sold. But this is a model, and it's driven by volume of product sold. We have the number of cups of lemonade sold; we could separate out internet sales versus sales from the card table in front of the house, and we could show the number of customers. But for now, let's keep it simple. I put a growth factor of 5 percent in the second column and multiplied sales each month by the constant growth factor of 5 percent.

b. I put the price on the second line. The price is constant from month to month. If you want to model how your income statement changes based on a change in price, you need the price on the spreadsheet.

c. Revenue is calculated on the spreadsheet by multiplying price and quantity. Some financial analysts put revenue calculation details right in the spreadsheet, some don't. In reality, even revenue is an estimate, because if someone promises to pay you (remember Bob from Fenway Park?), it might be revenue and it might be an increase in accounts receivable (A/R).

d. What is COGS? COGS stands for **cost of goods sold**. These are your variable costs—they vary with amount of product sold. It can also be called **cost of revenue** or other jargon.[48] This is what you paid for stuff you sold. In a business that sells a product, like a lemonade stand or a car manufacturer, COGS is relatively easy to calculate. To make lemonade you have lemons, you have sugar, you have vodka, you have cups. Wouldn't it be awesome if kids could have lemonade stands like that? Or to make automobiles you have steel, you have fake leather, you have cup holder parts, you have pre-crushed bits of snack foods, and so on.

When you have a service business such as consulting or being a hooker, it gets a bit trickier to calculate. For example, if a hooker rents a hotel room for a week and sees clients every night, is the room cost part of COGS? Certainly, the condoms are part of COGS. Condom usage varies up or down as production rises or falls. Hence, in economics these are called *variable costs*. But the room cost is the same whether she sees 10 johns a night or 1. So the room cost, which is the equivalent of office rent for, say, a software company, is not variable, and thus would not be part of COGS.

---

[48] I hate the word "jargon" almost as much as I hate jargon itself. The word "jargon" is of unknown origins, though some websites say it is an *onomatopoeic representation of birds* twittering. BTW, that last italicized clause is an awesome password. I used it for a while for my online bank account.

Generally, **COGS are variable costs**. This means that as you produce more, you spend more. An example is the lemon in lemonade. There's no way to produce more lemonade (of the same quality) without consuming more lemons. As you buy more lemons, your cost per lemon may stay the same, but the total expenditure on lemons will rise. Yes, I realize that if you buy enough lemons, you can get a bulk discount on the cost of lemons from the fruit distribution company, thus reducing the cost of lemons per glass of lemonade. I also realize that you're a fucking anal-retentive, nitpicker[49] if you think we are going to get that detailed at this point. Bite me.

e. Below the gross profit line are my fixed or overhead expenses. These are usually called **selling, general, and administrative** expenses in a financial model, or SGA. They can also be called *operating expenses* or other jargon (fuck, more jargon). In this case I predicted that every month, we made a new sign for $2. The hooker's hotel room would be considered SGA. She can reduce her SGA by doing in-calls instead of out-calls, and then she

---

[49] "Nitpicker" originally referred to someone who picks lice eggs—nits—from someone's hair.

could take a home-office deduction on her taxes, though she'd probably have to install home security cameras and pretend she's a "massage therapist" so her neighbors don't figure it out—business is complicated.

f. Earnings are revenue minus expenses. If you don't understand this, it doesn't mean you are blond, but it probably doesn't bode well for you.

An income statement starts with revenue and then cuts off pieces of it so that the amount of money flowing from the top line down to the bottom line is constantly shrinking. It's like a funnel.

Some of you are in sales and know all about the sales funnel. Or if you are in the internet space, they talk about conversion funnels. Or if you are working in a prison laundry, they use funnels to refill the smaller detergent bottles from big vats of detergent.[50]

Awesome craft-beer style infographic of an income statement:

---

[50] I totally made that up. I have no idea how prison laundries operate. When I think of prison, I think of the quote by Toombs in *The Chronicles of Riddick* about the Prison Planet Crematoria: "If I owned this place and Hell, I'd rent this place out and live in Hell."

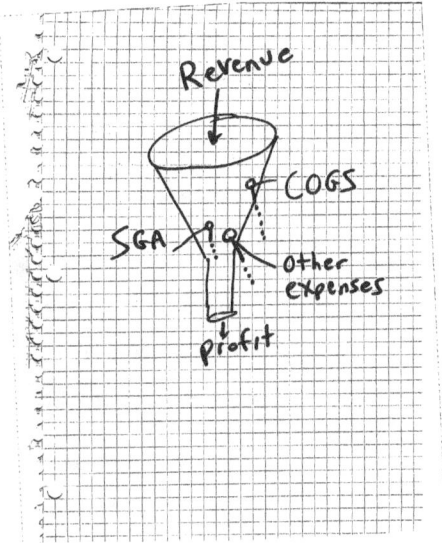

So you think that graphic is pretty awesome, huh? I got more where that came from, baby.

The Cash Flow Statement

The cash flow statement is the most difficult statement to understand but the easiest to calculate. The cash flow statement includes all cash that is coming into the company, whether it be[51] from revenue or from bank borrowing or selling things like stock. It also shows all the ways cash has left the company, including expenses such as salaries and making investments such as buying real estate. The cash flow statement is, in some ways, a means of adjusting the income statement to reflect changes in the balance sheet.[52] Or something.

Cash flow is a funny thing. Not funny *ha ha*, because that would be weird, but funny in the sense that it might appear to be redundant with income statements. Income statements also show money going in and coming out, right?

Uh, unfortunately, they are not the same.

The difference between income and cash flow, my young pup, is that not all of the money that goes into or out of your company is related to the goods and services your company produces. Sometimes that money is from the sale of equity or

---

[51] I believe this is an appropriate use of the subjunctive tense in English.

[52] If I am remembered for anything on earth, let it be for this sentence. Or alternatively, for the statement "You don't pay a prostitute for sex, you pay her to leave afterward." I've been told by many people that that is the most accurate description of prostitution they have ever heard. It also describes my marriage.

debt or other stuff. For example, if you sell an investor 50 percent of your company for $250,000, you must account for that money. But the proceeds from the sale of stock aren't revenue.[53]

On the cash flow statement., you account for all transactions that aren't related to operations—stuff that isn't the sale of goods and services.

Here are some other things that are accounted for on the cash flow statement that are not on the income statement.

- Buying large, long-term assets like real estate or equipment
- Borrowing money and paying back loans
- Paying dividends
- Raising capital

There are two common ways to present cash flow.

Cash Flow 1 has three types of cash movements:

- **Cash from operations** (income and expenses)
- **Cash from financing** (borrowing, selling shares)
- **Cash from investing** (stuff you can't expense like a

---

[53] The word *proceeds* is correctly treated as plural in this case, so if you think this is a grammatical error and the sentence should be "But the proceeds from the sale of stock *isn't* revenue," you can go suck eggs.

Learjet)

Cash Flow 2 has two types of cash movements:

- **Sources of cash** (everything coming in), like selling products or stock
- **Uses of cash** (everything going out), like paying salaries; buying cars, concert tickets, and dried-fruit snacks; and paying back loans

So here's how to calculate the three types of cash flow from the first method in a spreadsheet financial model (people who prefer the second method are out of luck.):

Cash from Operations: To calculate, simply start with your profit line (the last row of the income statement, the bottom line) and keep taking off non-cash stuff until you have cash from operations. In other words, you are actually "adding back" all the non-cash changes: if you have $150 in profit and that includes a depreciation charge (non-cash) of $50, then you add back $50 and your cash from operations is $200. Easy peasy.

Cash from Investments: This is where you account for stuff you are buying and keeping, like assets, corporate jets, cocaine to resell, dildos for board meetings, and so on. All assets you bought show up here. So, your purchase of a piece of machinery is shown against cash from investing—it's a negative number. This includes your signed and stained copy of *Delta of Venus* by Anais Nin: -$50,000. In addition, if you sell an asset, like a factory, or a 13-year-old Columbian girl, that cash shows up here as a positive number. (*Oh my fucking god, how could you say that?* – Don't worry, her mother tracks down the human traffickers, and, in 75 minutes of graphic gore, she kills them and their bosses, one by one, slowly, creatively, painfully, then forces their accountants to properly account for the loss of the rescued girl on the Income Statement. This is a non-cash charge against earnings because no money changed hands. Coming soon to your streaming services.)

When you sell an asset, you get two kinds of cash: return of principal, i.e., the initial purchase amount, and gain (or loss), i.e., the amount above (or below) what you paid. And if the asset has been depreciated, it gets more complicated. I might tell you about that later... or I might not... muhahahahaha.

Here's an example: You buy a cocaine purifying machine for $100. You don't count it as an expense. Instead, you *capitalize* it—meaning the value of the machine becomes an asset of the company. There's a chapter on that later. It doesn't appear on the income statement as an expense. It appears on the cash flow statement as an investment—a reduction in cash. And it appears on the balance sheet as an increase in long-term assets or investments.

Cash from investments will always show up as changes on your balance sheet as increases and decreases in your assets, like machinery, or poorly chosen trafficked young women with armed and dangerous mothers.

Cash from Financing: Here's where you record your equity infusions, your borrowings, and your debt payments. If someone gives you $1.2 million and you give them stock, you record it here. If you pay off a $30K loan, you record it here. Just imagine to yourself whether the money is going in or going out. If it's going in, you are increasing your cash from financing. If it is going out, you are decreasing your cash from financing. Whatever is bought or sold ends up on the balance sheet, as an asset or a debt.

The Balance Sheet

If you already know the basics of the balance sheet and you are sober, then you can skip to the naked pictures in the back of the book.[54] The balance sheet represents the financial state of the company at a specific moment in time. It is important to realize that the balance sheet of a company changes from day to day and moment to moment. It is usually prepared at a minimum of once per year.

Companies operate on a fiscal year, which is usually 12 months and probably ends at the end of a quarter (March 31, June 30, September 30, or December 31). But some companies, just to fuck you up, have fiscal years that end at other times. Salesforce.com, a company that's cool because I know some cool people who work there, ends its fiscal year on January 31 (or I think it does or maybe it did and no longer does and I don't really want to check or maybe I'm wrong).[55] Why? I don't have a clue, and I didn't ask.

At the end of the fiscal year, companies hire accountants to prepare financial statements. This process should be avoided by

---

[54] Made you look.
[55] I checked in March 2025 and it still ends on January 31.

the morally righteous among us. The rest should buy some popcorn and go watch. The balance sheet can take many months to prepare, so by the time it is prepared, it is already out of date. And that's why, when an accounting firm hands over an audited balance sheet to its client, the accountants usually are muttering things like "suckah," "gotcha," and "see you next week" under their collective breath.

The balance sheet has three basic components:

- Assets (stuff the company owns, minus any depreciation and plus any improvements, and money owed to the company)
- Liabilities (amounts the company owes to lenders)
- Equity (amounts the company owes to investors and profit or losses that have accumulated with dividends subtracted)

You are probably repeating your question "How do I tell the difference between equity and liabilities?" Or you might be saying, "I need another latte now." Or maybe you are praying for your life because captors are brandishing machetes and dancing around you and screaming in a foreign tongue. I don't know what you are doing. And do I care? Yes, I care, because maybe you are doing something really fun and I wasn't invited.

I'm never invited. FML.

Here's our basic balance sheet for our lemonade stand:

	Month 1	Month 2
Assets		
Cash (bank account)	10.00	20.50
Liabilities	0	0
Equity	0	0
Retained earnings	10.00	20.50
Liabilities + equity	10.00	20.50

The **cash** amount comes from the total change in cash calculation from the cash flow statement. As we bring in cash from the business, it goes into the bank account, or into the theoretical bank account that lives in our spreadsheet. If only we could access that account...

Retained earnings come from the profit line on the income statement. Basically, as you make money in your financial model, that money accumulates on the balance sheet as retained earnings. Retained earnings could also be called "all the money we've made so far that we haven't distributed to investors." As you bring in cash, that money accumulates in the balance sheet under cash. In this model, cash and retained earnings are the same number. In more complicated models where you pay dividends or have losses or invest profits in machinery, they will be different.

The Balance Sheet Equation

There is one equation that governs all accounting. In accounting books it is often called **the equation**; hence the title to this appropriately named section. In my original financial modeling tutorial on the Web, I always started by teaching how to create an income statement, but if you want to learn the basics of finance and don't need to build a financial model, then you could start with the equation, because much of accounting is derived from it.

assets = liabilities + equity

The balance sheet is just **the equation** writ large.

If you understand this, then WOOT! You are now a Third Degree Master Financier and you can learn the secret handshake and wear the funny hats!

This is an important equation to understand. It goes to the heart of the measurement of the value of a company at a s*pecific moment in time*. This equation does not explain whether a company is profitable or losing money. It doesn't explain or answer any questions about the future growth of the company. But it does provide a basis from which to make sure the accounting of the company is correct. And when you are building a working financial model, you can test it by seeing if the equation holds true.

If your balance sheet balances, you know it is correct.

Assets

The left side of the equation is pretty easy to understand. Assets are everything that the company owns. Assets are often listed as *current assets* and *long-term assets*. Current assets are typically those that can be turned into cash within one year. So a bank account, a six-month certificate of deposit, easy-to-sell inventory, and money owed to the company that will be paid soon are all current assets. In your own life, we often think of our next paycheck as a short-term asset—you can even go to one of those storefront finance places and borrow against your next paycheck with a paycheck loan, which is not the cleverest thing to do and is the financial equivalent of a drunken one-night stand. The terms on paycheck loans are really bad, but if you don't have a bank account or you need cash or you are in debt to a loan shark, that's what you do.

Long-term assets are everything else the company owns.

There's a lot of fudge factor on this stuff because the value of an asset, particularly a long-term asset, is pretty much a judgment call. You can hire appraisers to guess the value of an asset using their magic formulas and crystal balls or you can do it yourself, but it is all guesswork, though an educated guess is (probably) much better than having your toddler pound a calculator with your old MP3 player to come up with a number.

Some accounting rules require assets to be **held at cost,** meaning that if something like an antique vase was purchased for $1, then it needs to be on the balance sheet at $1, even if it is clearly worth $10,000. Other accounting rules require that assets be held at **lower of cost or market,** meaning that if something was purchased for $10 but the market price is obviously $5, then the asset needs to be listed on the balance sheet at $5. It's not generally *kosher* to increase the value of an asset on the balance sheet above cost unless it's quite clear that it will be worth that much for a long time. And there are rules about this stuff that are conveniently used to make people money in ways that are complex and devious.

The balance sheet isn't really supposed to be like your brokerage account, going up and down every day. That said, for the purpose of modeling you can do whatever the fuck you want. You have to be the moral decision maker of how you want to value your assets. There are probably tax issues. There are probably lots of issues. I can't come to your house and tell you what to do, but there are people who will do that, for a fee, often dressed in leather and holding a whip. I can't make that call for you. Angel, devil, angel, devil, truth, lie, truth, lie. Financial modeling is a morality minefield fraught with ethical dilemmas. Deal with it.

You want your model to be useful? Then put in numbers that make sense. You want a raise? Then make shit up so your model says what the bosses want to hear. You're a CPA? Then follow GAAP.

This does not mean that when you look at the balance sheet of some random company, you can assume that the asset portion is the real value of the assets of the company. You can't. It's all made-up shit. Yeah, that's right: Made. Up. Shit.

In the 1970s and 1980s there were many leveraged buyouts of companies that held large quantities of real estate assets on their balance sheets at cost. Asset values such as real estate had risen dramatically, so the balance sheet value or "book value" of the company's assets was far below what they were worth. Buyout firms bought these companies for as close to book value as they could (using money they borrowed) and then sold off the assets at the higher, prevailing market prices, reaping the rewards of better breeding, high-quality education, white privilege, and low morals. Life is good for evil financiers.

Don't overestimate the value of an appraiser, even if they

are just guessing. Their guess is probably better than your guess. The word "appraisal" comes from the word "prize," because if you get a good appraisal, it's like winning a prize. But I'm going to propose that the word "appraisal" comes from the word "guess" because it's anybody's guess what the stupid vase is worth.

Side note: For my divorce we needed to estimate the value of our house so that I could pay my ex-wife too much for it. Instead of hiring an appraiser, we looked on Zillow.com. We saved $250 on an appraisal and I paid $80,000 too much for the house.[56] Smooth move, *Ex-Lax.*

The right side of the equation is a bit more complicated. Let's start with liabilities. A liability is something we owe to a person or a company. One example is a bank loan. For example, if you have a company and you borrowed $15,000 from a bank to buy dog umbrella stands for your CEO,[57] you would have $15,000 on the liabilities side of the equation. You would also

---

[56] In a tiny, nearly insignificant bit of positive karma, the house then rose in value so much that I was able to stupidly invest in the auto-parts company that I hated.

[57] Dennis Kozlowski, former CEO of Tyco International, spent $15,000 of his company's money on "dog umbrella stands," whatever those are. Kozlowski was convicted of various financial crimes and spent some time in jail. He's now richer than you and a free man or he's dead of old age. Or both.

have $15,000 (of dog umbrella stands) in assets:

Assets: dog umbrella stands	$15,000
Liabilities: debt to bank	$15,000
Equity	$0

That's a very basic form of a balance sheet. Note that the amounts are equal.

I know I'm going to get hate mail,[58] but here it goes again: equity is (nearly) the same as liabilities. Instead of going to a bank for the $15,000 loan, let's say you went to your Uncle Mike and because he likes you, he invested $15,000 in the company and you gave him shares in the company. The equation still balances:

Assets: dog umbrella stands	$15,000
Liabilities	$0
Equity: Uncle Mike	$15,000

The fact is, and I've said this before, **you can't always tell the difference between equity and liabilities**. An investor could give you $1,000 but demand that he be paid back when you start making money and before you pay yourself. Well, that's

---

[58] I wish I got hate mail. I don't get any fucking mail.

pretty much what a lender does as well, so is the investor taking equity or debt? Hard to say, really. To many entrepreneurs, investor cash is the same as debt—they intend to pay it back whether the company makes money or not, because they are good hearted but not of sound mind. Of course, investors think the same way—that they'll be paid back regardless—so it all works out.

Private Equity

If you sell or buy equity (aka shares, stock, etc.) in a private company, your rights are far different from the rights you have if you buy or sell shares in a public company. With public company shares, your rights are (somewhat) supported by federal, state, and exchange rules that protect you, the investor, from being an idiot.

When you buy shares or lend money to a private company, you are pretty much on your own, a lone financial sailor adrift in a sea of sharks.

The terminology that defines when an investor or lender gets paid back is complex legal jargon. As they say, "the devil is in the details," and at no time is that truer than when dealing with investment contracts. When I started in finance, I was so naive, I thought that when we bought shares of a company, we'd get a little share certificate that we would keep in a manila file folder in the office. Turns out that's not true.

As an interesting anecdote, when I got canned from my job as an investment banker, the company's lawyer wanted my share certificate back, but I didn't have it. As far as I know, I never got one, but apparently they did exist. So somewhere there is a cardboard box, probably in the archives of some law firm, where my share certificate sits.

In fact, the shareholders' agreements, which are the true representation of ownership stakes in companies, are often 100-plus-page documents of dense legalese governing everything from how many board seats an investor has to the official mailing address for correspondence related to ownership.

And when I was in investment banking, many, many pages of statements by us and by the company repeated that we were who we said we were, we'd do what we said we'd do, and we owned what we said we owned. Those kinds of statements are called *representations and warranties* or, as shortened in legal and finance jargon, *reps and warranties*. A huge part of equity contracts are *reps and warranties*.

Here's an example of a stupid detail that caused me much anguish back in the day. In my first company, I raised a bunch of money. A total of $600,000 came from a single investor, a high-net-worth individual.[59] He initially promised $1 million. Then when his senior finance guys got into the act, the amount shrank and the terms shrank. The final deal was to give my start-up $120,000 per quarter for five quarters. For that $600,000 he got 40 percent of the company plus two board seats out of five.

---

[59] In finance that's what they call rich folks.

After making two payments totaling $240,000, my investor ran out of cash at his own company and couldn't make any more payments. I guess his net worth wasn't so high, eh?

He now owed my start-up $360,000. My start-up was now effectively in the position of lending him money (he owed us money, making us his lender). But the definitive agreements governing his shares didn't address what happened if he failed to pay, so he got to keep not only his 40 percent of the company while we fought over his missed payments, but his board seats. The documents should have made his shares and his board seats dependent on his payments. So he owned 40 percent of the company for a nice 60 percent discount.

Ross, a good friend of mine and investor, helped negotiate $25,000 from the investor so that I could pay off some corporate debts that I had personally guaranteed, but the lack of capital and my own ineptitude doomed that company, and everyone lost their investment. I had personally guaranteed the company's office lease; I used my unemployment insurance money to help cover that. After that I slowly spun down the financial toilet, ending up with $100,000 of credit card debt and a mortgage twice the size of my house purchase price. Eventually my next company, LandAndFarm.com, started making money, so it all worked out. Until I got divorced.

Lessons from all this:

- Make investors give you all the investment up front.
- Don't trust anyone.
- Always become friends with people named Ross.
- Never get married, never get divorced.

Liabilities Versus Equity

There are a few differences between equity and liabilities, but for financial modeling and understanding a balance sheet, the differences are not as great as you might think.

- A liability is an obligation that must be repaid.
- Equity carries no such obligation.[60]

If you borrow money from a bank, you must repay on terms agreed upon in the loan documentation. The lender gets paid set interest regardless of profitability.

If you take money from an investor, there is typically no

---

[60] You could actually stop reading at this point since everything else just explains those two bulleted sentences.

obligation to repay that money, but the investor then becomes a part owner of the company and shares in its profitability.

Equity gets the benefit of accumulated profit and losses. As a company makes more money than it needs to operate and pay its debt, the excess goes to the owners of the equity, as shown on the balance sheet in the item called *retained earnings* or *accumulated profit* or *CEOs' slush fund* or whatever. If a company loses money, the loss comes out of the equity holders' share on the balance sheet and might be called *accumulated losses* or *money my ex-wife will never take from me because I lost it*.

But in reality, there is a long continuum from equity to liabilities filled with exotic equity-like and debt-like instruments such as convertible bonds, warrants, equity with liquidation rights, and so on that make the actual calculation of how much is an *obligation* and how much is not an obligation to either an equity investor or a lender very complicated. Some shares might have more voting rights than other shares, even though they have the same economic value. Shares may be divided into *classes* or *series*. Shares can come with board membership rights, and debt can require that income be maintained at certain levels or that ratios of cash to assets be maintained at certain levels.

The goal of all these variations is to confuse you, the finance neophyte, and in turn, make other people rich. At least, that's my take on this. These structures certainly haven't been created to make life easier for anyone. Sure, investors need protection and banks need protection, but really, most of this stuff is done to make people other than you a lot of money.

Every possible permutation of ways you could think of for lenders and equity holders to screw each other has been tried. No reader of this book is evil enough to possibly compete with the slyness of the legal geniuses who put together the investment banking deals that create the debt and equity instruments of companies.

Finance Kōan: If you borrow $1 million from a bank and you can't pay it back, you are in trouble. If you borrow $1 billion from a bank and can't pay it back, the bank is in trouble.[61]

Though the terminology is complicated, the basic concept always holds true: all the equity plus all the liabilities when added together must equal all the assets of the company.

---

[61] A kōan is a kind of story or fable that a person should meditate on to fully grasp.

Enterprise Value

The equity and liabilities of a company, when added together, are referred to as the *enterprise value*. This is all the money that has gone into the company. It can be a useful gauge of how well the company has performed. For example, if $500 million in equity has gone into the company and $500 million in debt, then the enterprise value is $1 billion. And if the company has revenues of 27 cents per year and net assets of $43, then they aren't doing so well and you should not have invested even though he was your cousin.

And this fits with the equation.

assets (enterprise value) = equity + liabilities

Therefore

assets − liabilities = equity

But to fuck you up, they use more jargon.[62] For an

---

[62] Jargon makes Steve sad.

individual, you might talk about your "net worth." For a company, you talk about "book value" or "net asset value."

Company
assets − liabilities = **book value (equity)**

Individual
assets − liabilities = **net worth (equity)**

When you are doing these calculations for yourself personally, you use different jargon, but it's[63] the same thing. For example, if I want to know how broke I am, I add up all my assets, say $27, and subtract my liabilities, $75,000 in credit card debt. And this gives me my net worth of −$74,973.

It's all the same shit again. They use different words to confuse you, but book value and net worth are the same thing.

That said, we talked about the difference between equity and liabilities and how they are sometimes similar. In a company, when equity and liabilities look the same, it can be difficult to calculate book value. And that is why book value is not often a very good estimate of a company's value.

Net worth is **not** the same as enterprise value. Enterprise

---

[63] I typed "tit's the same thing" accidentally while writing this.

value is kind of like an estimate of everything that has gone into the company, whereas net worth is what would be left for the equity holders if they sold all the assets and paid all the debts.

Company

equity + liabilities = enterprise value = assets

assets − liabilities = **book value (equity) = net worth**

For an individual, enterprise value is kind of silly, because we don't sell portions of ourselves to others—we don't sell shares of our personal profit. Now, don't get all philosophical and tell me about how your employer owns your time and blah blah. I'm not going to get into a semantic argument about slavery and citizenship and all that crap. If you want to see a personal balance sheet, I've made one up below.

From a finance standpoint, one could argue that the government owns a percentage of your equity because it is entitled to a percentage of your profit through income tax. However, since no such structure is reflected on the balance sheet of corporate entities, despite having the same tax structure, it doesn't really make sense to think of the government as holding equity in you, though *Credit Rating Companies*[64] do,

---

[64] Like Standard & Poor's (S&P), Moody's, and Fitch Ratings.

actually, calculate the ability of a government to tax as part of their calculation of the probably that government debt will be paid back.

Side note on market capitalization: The market capitalization of the company is the sum of all the equity valued in the public market. Clearly, this can be calculated only if the company's stock is being traded publicly. Also, if the company has many types of shares, the market capitalization has to account for all of them. Market cap works better as a meaningful tool for companies with no debt. Private companies essentially have no market capitalization, but they have private values based on any sales of shares that have taken place, and that's basically the same thing as market cap.

Valuing Assets

Assets on a balance sheet can be valued in a variety of ways. Generally, as I said before, they are held at cost. But sometimes, especially if the public value has fallen, the company marks the value down. This is done on the income statement as a charge against earnings (non-cash). On the cash flow statement this loss would be added back. When a company takes its assets and changes the value on the balance sheet to reflect the market value, the process is called *marking to market*. How market value is determined is the subject of constant argument, because there's no real way to know market value until you sell the asset in question. So various means are used to appraise the value of assets, including paying appraisers tons of money, or using seers and soothsayers and dipping live animals into vats of wax or pouring boiling hot oil on unbelievers.

Basis

First, you need to know the word "basis." The basis of an asset is its value on the balance sheet, but sometimes it's not. More fucking jargon.

basis = net value = book value = value = cost = balance sheet value, et fucking cetera

When folks talk about basis, they are usually talking about tax basis, which is the original cost plus any capitalized expenses minus depreciation. I'll explain depreciation later.

Usually, if you have something valuable and put money into it by improving it or enhancing it, you account for that money by increasing the basis of the item. So the item had its initial cost, and then you put money into it, and its basis is now higher.

This matters when you go to sell the thing. The profit you get from the sale of the item is not the sale price minus the original cost, but the sale price minus the basis, which is the original cost plus the money you've put into the thing.

So if you have an asset, say a 1957 Facel Vega you bought for $200,000, and you add $1,000 in the form of a customized stereo, you could say your basis is $201,000. If you sell the car for $202,000, you make $1,000. You might tell your friends you made $2,000, but you know and I know that you made only $1,000.

Appraisal

I hear this all the time: "Appraisal is bullshit. Who the fuck knows what something is worth?"[65]

Actually, I wouldn't judge appraisal too harshly. Someone with knowledge of an asset class can guess at its value a heck of a lot better than someone with no knowledge. Appraisal is not all bullshit, but it's got a pretty high bullshit content.

I have a friend named Roy who is a car expert.[66] He's got a savant's knowledge of cars and car markets. He buys and sells exotic sports cars, beat-up jalopies, and pretty much everything in between. I was recently at his farm in Ohio and he had a vintage MG; two Camaro IROCs, one of which was set up for racing; a vintage dump truck; a rusting Model T; a Volkswagen Jetta modified to run on vegetable oil; and a half dozen more that I can't remember. It's kind of a hobby for him, but it's also his business.

And it turns out that knowing about cars translates into knowing about boats. He once saw a boat for sale in an IRS

---

[65] I don't hear this all the time. I've probably never heard it.
[66] He owns a 1957 Facel Vega.

auction and thought it might be a good deal. The boat was being auctioned on Cape Cod, which was an hour's drive from my house, so he called me up to go look at it.

The boat was a *Pearson True North*, and the minimum bid was listed as $63K. Roy did some research and told me it was worth between $120K and $130K, and we talked about me bidding up to around $85K so we could flip the boat and make some money. I hightailed my ass down to the marina where the auction was to take place. I stood in the back when the bidding started. I bid $85K. It sold for $130K.

So, it turns out that a knowledgeable person can accurately judge the value of an asset, but I still think most appraisals are bunk since most people are dumb as stumps.

There are six basic means of appraising an asset. And I'm summarizing here because appraisal is typically something passed from father to son and or taught at Hogwarts. It's really just magic, and you can use your brain as much as you want, but there's no actual way to determine the value of an asset unless you sell it, and even then you could sell it one day for $X and the next day for $X + 2. Appraisal is an edumacated guess, pure and simple.

Lifetime cost: This is the simplest and arguably the least accurate way to appraise an asset. You take what you originally paid for the asset, and then you add all the additional costs you've put into it. For example, if you buy a piece of machinery for $100 and every year you do $10 worth of repairs, after three years you could say that the value is $130. Of course—and here I'm going to give you a sneak peek at depreciation—the machinery degrades over time or it wouldn't need repairs, so perhaps its value declines by $10 every year because of wear and tear so the value is the same as when you bought it. Lifetime cost can also be used as the *tax basis* of an asset, which is the amount you effectively paid for the asset over its lifetime.

Replacement value: You can estimate an asset's value by calculating its replacement value—how much it would cost to build or buy such an asset at the present time. In the case of real estate, for example, you can't build more land; you have to buy it. To get replacement value you add up all the costs of the components of the asset or just take the value from your local machinery catalog or wherever. Replacement value should be fairly easy to calculate for something that is tangible and available elsewhere. Some assets have no realistic replacement value. If you have a customer list or something intangible like your brand, there is no easy way to establish a replacement value and you have to rely on magicians called *appraisal consultants* who live in a dark place far away in the magic kingdom of Cash Cow.

Comparable sales: You can estimate the value of an asset by looking at similar assets that have sold within a reasonable time frame—say, within the last six months or year, or even a day if the asset is very liquid. This is commonly used for real estate appraisals.

Net present value: If an asset generates income (say, an apartment building or a bond), you can calculate the net present value using mathematics. The sum of the future cash flows that flow from the asset to the asset's owner over its expected life can be a reasonable estimate of what someone will pay for it. The math for this can be very complicated. However, there is a super easy shorthand and I'm going to give it to you because you got this far in the book.

If something generates $10,000 every year, and the discount rate of future cash flows is 7%, then value of the asset is 10,000/.07 or $142,857.14. That's it.

Equation for present value of a perpetuity:

Annual income (or yield)/Discount Rate = Present Value

This equation fails if the discount rate is changing over time or the cash coming in stops at some point.

Buyer estimates: It is possible to simply solicit non-binding bids from buyers for the asset. In some cases, you might have a written bid from a buyer that you didn't accept. That would certainly be a basis for value if you thought the buyer was serious.

Market value: Some stuff, such as stocks and bonds, have a liquid market. To get the value, you simply use the existing market value. No need for fancy footwork with these.

Note that these various appraisal methods overlap. A replacement cost might be the same as a comparable sale for a custom item such as a painting. The lifetime cost and net present value are flip sides of the same thing—one looks to the past, and the other looks to the future.

Companies can easily use their balance sheet to confuse and confound investors. For example, if two companies own identical apartment houses and one company adjusts the value of its apartment house every year on its balance to reflect market value but the other company uses only the original cost, the balance sheet of the two companies may be very different despite the fact that they hold identical assets.

GAAP has rules about how assets are required to be valued

on a balance sheet and the circumstances under which one can increase or decrease their value. Different countries, as well, have different rules about this. Forests, for example, are often held at cost in the United States even though tree growth is incontrovertibly increasing the value of the forest every year. In New Zealand, where I was involved in the purchase of many hectares of planted *pinus radiata*, the forests were often revalued every year, with the gains shown on the balance sheet.

The Dreaded Pie Analogy

All financial lectures have a pie analogy hidden somewhere in them, where you talk about splitting up the pie and who owns how many slices. This is an old tradition dating back to the dawn of mankind when our hunter-gatherer selves would stalk the herds of pie through the African veld, waiting patiently for the chance to strike down a young and vigorous pie and harvest nutritious pie innards. And I continue this tradition here, today, just like my ancestors did before me.

No, fuck that. Pie analogies are stupid.

Accrual Accounting Vs. Cash Accounting

So this brings up the difference between accrual and cash accounting. Well, it doesn't, but I didn't have a good transition, so here goes. The difference between accrual and cash accounting greatly affects whether you have a profit, so we need to get a handle on what it means.

Cash Accounting:

Cash accounting is for people who trust nobody. For example, coke dealers and hookers.

When you use cash accounting, you calculate all your financial variables on what you have in your pocket or bank account in cash only. When I was starting LandAndFarm.com, I had no money. Nothing. In fact I had negative money. My net worth was below zero. I didn't buy socks for two years. I cancelled my health insurance. I borrowed my mortgage payment on my credit cards every month. Every day I would get up and know that the only money I had in the world was the money I had in my pockets. And when I went to bed, the same was true—everything I had was in my pockets,[67] except that my pajamas had no pockets, which was fine because I had no money anyway. I lived in a cash world. Bills were paid when I had the cash. Money that was promised to me was ignored until it was in my bank account. This is cash accounting. If you are a hooker, it's probably the same: you don't care about promises, only about crisp or soggy bills handed to you before you take off your bra. Street-level cocaine dealers are the same: they have coke and cash, and everything else is basically not worth anything. Until someone actually pays for their drugs, you don't count their cash. Cash is king.

Accrual Accounting:

Accrual accounting has to do with trust and is the entire basis of our financial system, but that's not something we can discuss within the scope of this book because it's a really boring subject.

When you use accrual accounting, you get to count as revenue money that has not yet been paid to you but has been promised.

So if you are a lawyer and you perform 100 hours of legal

---

[67] I cannot say or write or read the word "pockets" without thinking "What has he gots in his pocketses?" Thank you, J.R.R. Tolkien, even if I have the quote wrong.

work for someone and you bill them and give them 30 days to pay you, you book that as revenue if you use accrual accounting. If you charge $700 per hour and they owe you $70,000 (seriously, lawyers make bank!), you can enter $70K[68] into your financial software as revenue. Unfortunately, if your client doesn't pay you by the end of the year, you may need to pay taxes on it even before you receive it. Bummer. (So you don't bill them until the next tax year... That's a tax tip from your uncle Steve.)

That also works for expenses. Under cash accounting, if you buy something but haven't paid for it, then it isn't counted as an expense. But under accrual accounting, if you've been billed for it, it is an expense.

So over the course of a month, if you sell a bunch of stuff— say you sell four shipping containers full of gallon bottles of a product called SunLube™ (a personal lubricant and suntan lotion)—and some folks have paid you and some haven't, you can't calculate your profit until you decide what counts as revenue and what doesn't.

And if your sales of SunLube™ are in July and everyone

---

[68] Financial folks often put a "K" at the end of a number to indicate thousands, so $30K = $30,000. This is an abbreviation for "kilo," which is a Latin prefix meaning 1,000. K? Note, I first started using "K" for 1,000 when I was young and played Dungeons and Dragons with my friend Alex. We used to count our copper, silver, and gold loot using "K" so if our party of adventurers killed a dozen orcs and opened a chest, it might contain 6K copper, meaning 6,000 copper pieces. And they say D&D is bad for you.

pays you in October because you allow your customers 90 days to make payment, then your revenue on a cash basis could be $0 for July since nobody has paid you yet even though you received orders for $1 million of SunLube™ lotion. But on an accrual basis, you would book $1 million in revenue in July.

The process of deciding when to book revenue, when you don't actually have that revenue in your bank account, is called *recognizing revenue*. And businesses play lots of games with the recognition of revenue.

If you sell things like software license agreements and your customers pre-pay for a year at a half-off discount midway through your fiscal year, then your revenue calculations could be quite complicated. There are all kinds of accounting rules regarding when to recognize revenue under accrual accounting. I don't know all those rules, but basically if it increases how much you owe in taxes, then you probably are doing it right.

And there are tons of great ways to mess around with revenue by playing games with sales. An acquaintance of mine was a lawyer for a Fortune 100 retailer. She was in charge of negotiating software licenses from vendors who sell software like the stuff that runs those scanners at checkout. Every December the salespeople from the vendors started pushing very hard to get contracts signed so that the revenue could be booked for that year and thus increase their bonuses. A two-week delay of a closing into January could mean a 12-month delay in a bonus.

Ha Ha

Ha. I've done nothing at all to explain EBITDA. All I've done is explain how ridiculously complicated it can be to calculate revenue. I've suckered you, and I've already recognized the revenue from the sale of this book. Am I Mr. Smart or what? Finance is like an onion wrapped inside an enigma inside a riddle inside a fortune cookie inside a dog.[69]

There are tricks companies play with the recognition of revenue to mess around with their earnings. And you can try to understand this, but really it will be very difficult for the average Joe or Jane or Abu or Abbie or Rover or whatever your name is to be able to look through an EBITDA calculation and figure out whether the company is recognizing revenue early to pump earnings or has held back recognizing revenue so that earnings pop next year when the board of directors' stock vests. What? You don't think companies pull that bullshit? Wake up, Grandma, the world is ugly.

I used to be a stock options trader in Chicago at the Chicago Board Options Exchange. I sucked at it. Everything I bought went down. Everything I sold went up. But with options

---

[69] Outside of a dog, a book is a man's best friend. Inside of a dog, it's really dark. —Groucho Marx

sometimes you can make money when things go against you. All you need is what we called *edge*—that's the small percentage difference you get over the public by being a market maker. So if an option was quoted at 1 to 1½[70] and you wanted to sell, you'd be selling to me for 1, and if you wanted to buy from me, you'd be paying me 1½. In theory the true price of the option was 1¼, so the edge I got was ¼. But regardless, if I paid 1, then probably the market would move and the next bid or offer on that option would be ⅝ to ⅞. My good friend and successful equity trader Ross told me once, "The stock market is made for suckers. You are a sucker." Only your friends can be that honest.

My point is that finance is the same way: it's made for suckers, and that's you. P. T. Barnum would have been brilliant on Wall Street if the circus thing had failed.

Example: If you are looking at a manufacturer of something large, like airplanes, and they say their revenue is $4 billion, the fact is that unless you actually go and look at the contracts for the airplanes, you can't be sure if that $4 billion is really going to come in. There are probably a dozen or even a hundred provisions in the contracts for those airplanes that would allow the buyers to walk away long before they've paid more than a tiny deposit.

---

[70] Here's how old I am. Options are no longer quoted in fractions but in decimals, so the market nowadays would be 1 to 1.5.

I don't have a solution for this problem. Wall Street investment banks that are analyzing the stock and promoting it to their clients have the ability to figure out how accurate the revenue statements of the company are, but they have a strong incentive to lie to make it look like the company is doing really well since they get big investment banking fees from the companies.

So, with that depressing news, let's move on.

In most businesses, you need to pay taxes or you may need to plan for some future event or you just want to know what the hell is going on. So you need to calculate your profit over a period of time, regardless of whether you sell one item or millions of items. Or perform a single service for one client or for many clients.

I had a toy company for a short period of time that failed. Go figure. By the time the business was really on the ropes, I knew I had to bring in some real revenue. And the reality is that a simple way to bring in revenue is to raise prices. Of course, when you do this, you shrink your sales (usually). So I changed my business goal from selling 1,000 sets of toy blocks for $29.95 to selling a single set of toy blocks for $3 million. Sadly, that strategy failed.

Fun Game

Read this book aloud with friends. Drink every time someone reads a footnote.

Less Fun Game

Read this book aloud with friends. Drink every time someone reads the word "diverticulitis."

Another Game

Read this book alone. Drink every time you see a punctuation mark.

Capitalizing Expenses

So, this is really the puckering anus of financial jargon. The termed *Capitalized Expense* really means *It's Not A Fucking Expense, It's An Investment, Yeesh.*

When you buy something and **consume** it, the cost of the item is subtracted from your revenue. This is reflected on the income statement as an **expense**. If the item has a useful life longer than your accounting period, the part you didn't consume should be put on the balance sheet and only what is consumed should be expensed. The part that is not expensed is *capitalized*, meaning added to the balance sheet.

But of course, it's not quite that simple. If you buy a box of a dozen pens and use only 1 per year, what do you do about the cost of the other 11 pens?

Answer: You don't fucking worry about them—the number is too small. If you buy 100 million pens, it becomes a problem, but until then you simply expense the box of pens and just use them whenever you want, knowing they've already been *accounted* for. It's a problem to expense something you don't use only if you derive value from it over a long period (a piece of machinery) or you're going to sell it (inventory).

Things you shouldn't fully expense, but should capitalize:

- Stuff that lasts much longer than your accounting period (machinery, cars, and intangible assets like patents and websites)

- Stuff you are going to sell much later than the end of the accounting period (inventory and parts)

Basically, stuff you expense isn't added to the balance sheet. But stuff you capitalize is added to the balance sheet, under *investments* or *capital* or *assets* or *inventory* or *stuff we own*.

Spending money results in one or both of two possibilities:

1. The money is gone and you used or consumed the item. (You bought an apple and ate it. This is an expense.)
2. The money is gone and you have something in return that you are keeping. (You bought an apple and it's on your kitchen counter. This is an investment in inventory, say.)
3. There are no other options.

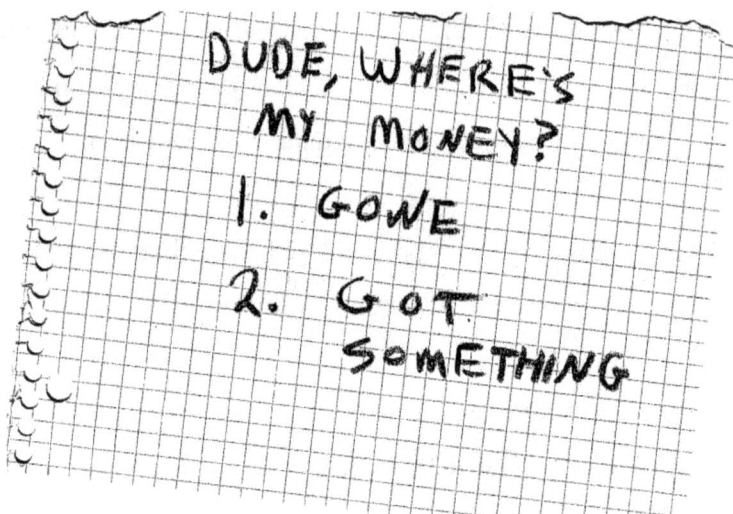

Let's classify some purchases:

	Gone (Expense)	Got Something (Capitalized)
Buying porn online	✓	
Buying food for your fridge		✓
Buying food at a restaurant	✓	
Paying mortgage interest	✓	
Paying mortgage principal		✓
Losing $5 at craps	✓	
Giving your mistress rent	✓	
Buying a private jet		✓
Buying health insurance	✓	

In the case of "got something," the money must appear on your balance sheet in some other form. It doesn't matter what you bought or what it is—if you don't expense it, if you capitalize it, the item must appear on your balance sheet.

For financial modelers this is important because expenses appear in only one place in the model: the income statement.

Costs that are capitalized show up in the cash flow statement, probably under *cash for investing* and then appear under *assets* in the balance sheet.

Depreciation, Depletion, Amortization, and Orgasms

Depreciation is such a wacky concept, it deserves its own chapter. And let me say that once you *get* depreciation and its sick siblings, depletion and amortization, you'll be in the top .01 percent of humans measured by their understanding of finance. Now, for those of you who like to be tested, here's a multiple-choice question:

Depreciation is

A. a means of accounting for wear and tear on fixed assets.
B. something accountants dreamed up to fit purchases made over one time period to multiple time periods.
C. a great way of avoiding taxes.
D. further evidence that accounting and necromancy are one and the same.
E. the punch line of a joke you heard in a bar about an investment banker's willy.
F. all of the above.

Please completely fill in the circle that corresponds to your answer:

Ⓐ Ⓑ Ⓒ Ⓓ Ⓔ Ⓕ

If you chose anything but F, you should probably reconsider your career choice. Perhaps something in the automotive-safety testing industry would suit you better?

Depreciation works like this: Say you are a cocaine dealer and you buy a *Learjet* for $1 million. You put "*Learjet—$1,000,000*" as a long-term asset on your balance sheet. You also put "*Learjet—$1,000,000*" under "cash for investing" on your cash flow statement for the period when you bought the jet.

You have a busy year and fly all over the country, including a jaunt to the Midwest during a storm where the plane has to be put down in a hayfield, but you are okay and have scrumptious homemade apple pie at the farmer's house and meet his daughter, who turns out to have an awesome voice and you back her first record and the rest is country music history. The plane gets heavily used by other folks as well. Your daughter holds her sweet sixteen party in it, and a bunch of your son's friends puke during a kegger he has in it. Your *Learjet* is no longer worth $1 million. It has depreciated in value. So who gives a flying hedgehog turd if it went down in value? Answer: You do.

There are many reasons why you might want to accurately reflect the new, depreciated value on your balance sheet. One of the best reasons to account for depreciation is, drum roll, please... taxes.

Since the value of something you own has declined, you have lost money. Businessmen since the dawn of time have held that you should be able to deduct losses from taxable income. Therefore, they record depreciation as a loss on their income statements. But since it's not real money that's been lost—just the value of an asset being held, something you already bought and accounted for—it's a *non-cash expense* against earnings.

So, let's say your *Learjet* declined in value by $100K. You can put an expense item called "depreciation" on your income statement and reduce your earnings by $100K. You just reduced your taxes! By buying a *Learjet*! Whooeee! So think about this: if you can get a bank to finance your jet and your payments are less than depreciation in a year when you have a high tax bill, then you can actually walk away with more cash at the end of the year by buying a private jet.

In fact, the more expensive the thing you buy, the more and the longer you can reduce your taxes by the amount of the depreciation. This is why the rich continually get richer and never pay their fair share of taxes. I know, I sound like a fucking socialist, latte-drinking, limousine liberal, douche-canoe. Well, work in high finance and travel in the most impoverished places on Earth, and you'll be just like me.

Some of you now understand depreciation. The rest of you are normal humans. Let's take the example of the *Learjet* and put it on a couple of balance sheets. The first balance sheet is at the beginning of the year, and the second balance sheet is at the end of the year. We are showing only the long-term assets part of the balance sheet to keep the information noise level down.

BALANCE SHEET Beginning of Year		BALANCE SHEET End of Year	
Learjet	1,000,000	*Learjet*	1,000,000
		Depreciation	(100,000)
Total assets	1,000,000	Total assets	900,000

This is pretty simple, right? We own a *Learjet*. It declined in value because of the puke stains on the seats and that bumpy landing in a cornfield in Iowa, so it's worth less than it was when we bought it.

Now the question arises of how to financially model the $100,000 reduction in asset value. Answer: On your income statement as well as the balance sheet as well as the cash flow statement. You didn't really spend $100,000. Nor did you really lose that money from your bank account. It just disappeared. It's gone. Like your virginity on that hot summer night in the backseat of an '83 Taurus—gone.

So we do the same in accounting. Only in accounting it's not called a "burning hot memory used for fantasy purposes during a disintegrating marriage." Instead, it is called a *non-cash charge against earnings*, which is really an expense that wasn't paid in cash.

Below is part of an income statement. I'm showing the revenue with the depreciation charge. This is how much money you brought into the company minus your loss on the value of your jet.

Income Statement
1 Year

Revenue from cocaine sales	5,000,000
Depreciation of *Learjet*	(100,000)
Taxable earnings	4,900,000

I want you to remember this phrase *non-cash charge against earnings*, because if you use it during casual conversation outside of work, you might very well lose friends; be careful. Non-cash expenses are the numbers that really mess up folks when they read financial statements. Non-cash doesn't necessarily mean no cash moved around, but it means that we are adjusting something on the balance sheet. And that adjustment will show up on the income statement and the cash flow statement.

Okay, we had earnings of $4.9 million, but we actually got more cash than that, right? We actually got $5 million in cash. But we reported only $4.9 million to the tax authorities since they allowed us to write off $100,000 in depreciation expenses on our *Learjet*.

There's a way to make sure that the actual cash we have is totaled somewhere so that when you report to your superiors in Medellin or Juarez, you report the right number, since it's different from the amount of earnings we are reporting. We do this on the cash flow statement.

So here it is:

Cash Flow
1 Year

Earnings (from income statement)	4,900,000
Add back depreciation	100,000
Change in cash—cash flow	5,000,000

And *voila*! The cash flow statement shows exactly how much cash we actually got from sales during the year. The *change in cash* is, to some extent, a much better indication of how the business did during the year than the income statement. And this is why investors who like to sell their skills are always talking about cash flow this and cash flow that. Cash flow reflects what actually happened to the bank account much more accurately than income does.

Depletion is next, yo.

Seriously, depletion is ignored by the press and the term isn't widely used, but it's important... to me. It's not going to be important to you, so you can skip to the next chapter if you can find it. I have a soft spot for depletion since it's something I dealt with as a forester. Plus, you might come across it one day. And if you meet a mining accountant and you think he or she is cute and you want to impress them, you can toss out your knowledge of depletion.[71]

So if you go exploring for gold and spend $100K on exploration and find a gold mine and buy mining rights for $900K from the landowners, and then you extract gold and sell the gold, you can actually avoid taxes on your initial $100K exploration costs. Maybe you were not allowed to expense the exploration costs, the government made you capitalize them, and

---

[71] Wearing some tight jeans wouldn't hurt either.

they went on your balance sheet as part of the value of the mine.

There is an assumption that the amount of gold in the mine is finite and that as you extract gold from the mine, the amount of gold is *depleted*. The amount of depletion allowed is determined by the tax overlords.

Depletion looks something like this:

BALANCE SHEET Beginning of Year		BALANCE SHEET End of Year	
Gold mine cost	900,000	Gold mine cost	900,000
Capitalized expenses	100,000	Capitalized expenses	100,000
		Depletion	(100,000)
Total assets	1,000,000	Total assets	900,000

It's really the same as depreciation—you have an asset and you mine it, cut it, use it, abuse it, burn it, eat it, whatever, and it's now worth less than when you bought it. And this use/abuse of your asset takes place over an extended period of time, exceeding a single accounting period, so you can reduce your income by the depletion amount.

Amortization—A Short Story

Amortization means "a little death," And *la petite mort* also means "a little death" and *la petite mort* is used as an allegorical stand-in for orgasm. And that's about as close you'll ever get to sex when practicing finance.

Amortization also translates roughly as "deathification." You pay for your big expense not at the moment of the purchase, but slowly, over time, each payment is a tiny cadaverous instantiation of your financial life—a bit of hard-earned value lopped off like a pinky or a toe by a mob enforcer, reminding you that you are not in control; you are owned by others and you are dying with every payment. Nickle and dimed. A thousand paper cuts. Bled.

In olden times, to buy a house folks would borrow money from a bank and pay interest but no principal for many years and then pay the loan principal back in one lump sum.

Then an evil person came up with the idea that folks should pay back some of the principal of the loan every month along with the interest. Thus *amortization* of loans was born. And each month 1 billion people[72] on earth pay down loans, amortizing the loans over their lifetimes until they die lonely and broke. The

---

[72] I have no idea how many people pay amortized loans. I'm just making shit up at this point.

math behind amortization tables is difficult. And there's no real shortcuts that work. This is why we have computers.

If you buy something expensive, you might not be able to expense it all at once. And, the government won't let you. Plus, if it remains in your possession, it wasn't "expended." So amortizing the cost makes sense.

Some of it can be recognized as an expense each year so that eventually it will be fully accounted for, and that's amortization—a small expense, a little death, each accounting period until the item in question is fully amortized—dead.

There's some logic to amortization, particularly if you are buying something that has a limited useful life but is an "intangible" asset, such as a customer list. Customer lists eventually become stale as customers move, die, age, change tastes, or otherwise become something other than good customers. Patents are also amortized because they have a limited life. License agreements that expire and other similar contracts that have value now but decline over time are often amortized.

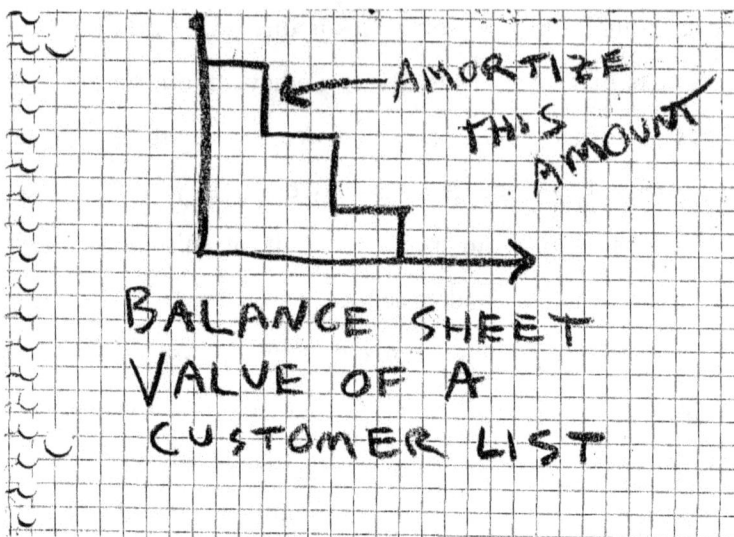

AMORTIZE
THIS
AMOUNT

BALANCE SHEET
VALUE OF A
CUSTOMER LIST

So amortization and depreciation are nearly the same thing. So why don't **they** call amortization depreciation? Answer: Because **they** suck and **they** want you to be confused and poor.

If the devil bought your soul, he'd probably amortize it. Because your soul is probably going to burn in hell for less than eternity since only murderers and rapists and authors burn for eternity and you aren't any of those things. (Please don't email me and correct me on this one.) Others go back to earth as CPAs and politicians. You will probably burn in hell for just a few hundred years or so and then you'll be absorbed into the cosmic anti-matter of the universe to be reconstituted as a dung beetle or an oyster.[73]

So every accounting period, assuming the devil does accounting and assuming his accounting periods are, say, a year, he would put souls he purchased, such as mine, on his balance sheet as an asset. To account for whatever he spent on them instead of expensing the entire cost in the first year, he would assign a smaller cost each year until the souls were fully amortized.

---

[73] "You are a very troublesome little fellow. I think I should teach you one of my special lessons. What do you think, Robert? Benson? What would look nice? Half-warthog? Half-donkey? Half-oyster? Half-carrot?" —Evil, *Time Bandits*

How to Cheat on Your Taxes

Actually, if you are smart—and I think you probably are smart because you aren't me, and you decided to read this book instead of write it—you probably realize that the government doesn't actually let you determine the depreciation on your assets. Why not? Because if we let companies set their own depreciation, they'd probably wait until they had a lot of revenue one year and then depreciate as much as they could, which would reduce their taxable income. And in years when they had lower revenue and perhaps had losses, they'd depreciate very little. This is how companies can manipulate their taxable income with depreciation and why the government is so particular about depreciation rules.

See below: by depreciating the *Learjet* ($1,000,000 cost) faster, we save money in taxes.

10-Year Depreciation of Jet

Income Statement

1 Year

Revenue from cocaine sales	5,000,000
Depreciation of *Learjet*	(100,000)
Taxable earnings	4,900,000
Tax @ 35%	(1,715,000)
Earnings after tax	**3,285,000**

2-Year Depreciation of Jet

Income Statement

1 Year

Revenue from cocaine sales	5,000,000
Depreciation of *Learjet*	(500,000)
Taxable earnings	4,500,000
Tax @ 35%	(1,575,000)
Earnings after tax	**3,425,000**

SCORE! We saved $140,000 in taxes by depreciating the entire *Learjet* in 2 years versus 10 years.

So there are long, complicated depreciation rules governing how quickly or slowly you can depreciate an asset. Most folks want to depreciate assets fast so that they can get the tax benefit immediately, whereas the government wants you to depreciate things slowly so that they get more in taxes. If the government had its way, nothing would be depreciable and everything you spend would go on your balance sheet as an asset and you'd pay taxes on all your revenue. And we would all be sad sacks.

However, if you are not profitable, then perhaps you might want to play around a little with the depreciation as much as the law will allow and perhaps a little more than that (wink, wink[74]) so that you depreciate things slowly at first and then more when you have the chance.

You can always accelerate your depreciation by selling the item in question. If the remaining balance sheet value of the item or the tax basis is greater than what you sold it for, you record a loss on the sale and take that loss.

Now, I'm not recommending you do this, but if your assets don't depreciate fast enough according to the tax code, you could sell them to "a friend" who might lease them back to you. You'd record a loss on the sale. So if you have a lot of income one year and you need to replace some equipment, that would be a good year to do it if your existing equipment isn't depreciated but its value is low. The tax savings from the write-off of the loss on the sale of the old equipment could pay for new equipment.

In fact—and here's where the light bulb should go on for you—imagine if you purchased an asset and depreciated the asset by 100 percent in the first year. That would effectively make the purchase the same as an expense.

An expense is simply something that is consumed during the time period of the income statement, whereas an investment is

---

[74] "Yes. Nudge nudge. Snap snap. Grin grin, wink wink, say no more." — Eric Idle, Monty Python's Flying Circus

something that is only partially used up during the accounting period, and the amount by which it is used is depreciation.

The key is realizing that depreciation is related to all three financial statements. The beginning values and ending values of the asset being depreciated are on the balance sheet. The depreciation itself is subtracted from the income statement and the amount is added back on the cash flow statement.

Depreciation rates are set by the IRS, since depreciation's entire *raison d'être* is perpetuated by the tax benefits that one derives from it.

The rules governing depreciation rates, including accelerated depreciation rates, are called the "Modified Accelerated Cost Recovery System," or MACRS. Google away on that shit.

I don't know all the rules, but when I do financial modeling, I figure 3 years for high technology—stuff like computers—7 to 20 years for plant and equipment, and 30 years for buildings. You are not supposed to depreciate land, which is why so many companies will value land low and buildings high when they purchase land and buildings. Those tax cheats! Go ahead and make up your own rules if you're too lazy to ask an accountant. The IRS will also be happy to calculate your depreciation for you if you want: they know you're going to make up half the fucking numbers anyway, you lazy good-for-nuttin'!

To model depreciation, I put it on its own spreadsheet or tab. I generally call that spreadsheet *depreciation* because I once called my depreciation spreadsheet "Long Dong Silver" and had to attend sensitivity classes at work.[75]

---

[75] Kidding. I never attended any sensitivity classes.

Profit, Retained Earnings, and Dividends

When modeling a company, folks often build in profit. Very few folks will build a financial model that shows monthly losses forever. Usually they make themselves rich in the spreadsheet—rich enough to buy a house in Palo Alto and a purebred Pekinese named Mindy and another house in Palo Alto for Mindy. Usually the profit just piles up in the "cash" line of the balance sheet. And this is okay, but it means your balance sheet won't balance—your "equity + liabilities" won't equal your assets.

So accountants have created a portion of equity called "retained earnings," which is really just the accumulated profit of the company. For a balance sheet to balance, as profit accumulates and the short-term asset side of the balance sheet grows, we simply add that excess to retained earnings. And if you pay out profit (called "dividends"), you add a line on the balance sheet called "dividends" and subtract that from retained earnings.

A dividend reduces the equity of a company. Accumulated profit increases the equity of the company. A sample balance sheet is below just to show how these things could look.

BALANCE SHEET

End of Year

Short Term Assets (cash)	5,000,000
Long Term Assets (factory)	900,000
Total Assets	**5,900,000**
Loan from rich friend	1,000,000
Total Liabilities	**1,000,000**
Initial equity from rich friend	1,000,000
Retained Earnings	4,900,000
Dividends Paid	(1,000,000)
Total Equity	**4,900,000**
Equity+Liabilities	**5,900,000**

WTF Is EBITDA?

Glad you asked. Cash flow is sometimes called EBITDA or Earnings Before Interest, Taxes, Depreciation, and Amortization. Frankly, I think interest and taxes should be not be removed from estimates of cash flow, but who am I?

What we are trying to get at is "Is this company making money?" And as you are beginning to realize, there are a hundred different answers to that question, so you choose a metric[76] and stick to it. Some folks use a term called "free cash flow," (FCF) which is usually *cash from operations*, though some folks use FCF and EBITDA interchangeably. Those people can mow my bat lawn, Robin.

One primary purpose of calculating EBITDA is to figure out how much cash the company generates that would be available to pay interest on debt. Interest is tax deductible, so we want to make this calculation before paying taxes. Depreciation and its ilk are non-cash, so we want to make this calculation before depreciation et al. And finally, we calculate EBITDA before interest because we want to know the total available to

---

[76] A metric is another word for "measurement" that geeks and business people use to further separate us from the common folk—again the use of jargon to perpetuate the class struggle.

pay all interest due.

The goal of EBITDA is to find out if we can use the company's own cash flow to borrow enough money to buy the company. Yeah, that's pretty wacked, but that's what financiers do—they use other people's money to make themselves money.

In investment banking there is a saying, *Use other people's debt to buy your equity.* That's basically how investment banks make money. They borrow money, they buy companies. The companies earn more than the debt payments or have assets greater than the debt. The net result: the investment banker or his clients make enough money to pay for a colonoscopy in the United States.

So, if you look at an income statement, you should see *revenue* at the top and some kind of final profit line on the bottom after various expenses are subtracted. These expenses should include interest paid on debt, depreciation, and taxes. Rather than try to find the right number somewhere in the middle of the income statement, financial analysts simply add back interest, taxes, and depreciation (and amortization) to the final profit number to get EBITDA.

So really, EBITDA should stand for *Profit with Interest, Taxes, Depreciation, and Amortization Added Back In* or PWITDAAABI, but that would be really silly sounding, much sillier than EBITDA.

Random EBITDA Examples

So, just to be clear, this isn't rocket surgery that only certified Wall Street geeks can understand. Below, you'll see an income statement. This is from a well-known company that I won't name.[77] As a newly anointed expert, you'll recognize the descriptions of the line items. Sales is at the top. You can see Depreciation and Amortization. You can see interest payments.

	Fiscal Year End Jan 31, 2024
Net Sales	86,377
Cost of sales	5,7533
Gross margin	28,844
Expenses	
SGA	15,570
Deprec/Amort	1,717
Operating income	11,557
Interest - net	1,382
Pre-tax earnings	10,175
Tax provision	2,449
Net earnings	7,726

And here's the spectacular stupidity of modern finance in

---

[77] Lowes, 2023 Annual Report, page 51

black and white.[78] How many fucking terms do these douche canoes use for profit?

1. Gross margin
2. Operating income
3. Pre-tax earnings
4. Net earnings

Seriously? And these are probably nice young accountants with scrubbed faces, valuable degrees from good schools, and families and barbecues and among them only a single arrest for marijuana possession in the last three years. But holy shit, Batman, can you get more obfuscatory?[79]

Anyway, I'm not bothered by this at all.

To calculate EBITDA, we take the Net earnings (7,726), and then add back in Interest (1,382), Taxes (2,449), and Depreciation and Amortization (1,717) and we get:

EBITDA: 13,274

Now, if you search the web for 2024 Lowes EBITDA, the

---

[78] If you download the annual report, the income statement has a blue background.

[79] Mic drop

answer is slightly different. I got 13,480 from some random data-sucker web site that had more popup ads than my favorite porn site. I have no idea why that number is different. Might be the actual taxes paid were different. Or maybe there's a note in the financial statements that clarifies the depreciation. Could be that site just sucks moose ass. Could be anything. But, I know this: the accountants who wrote this annual report are paid more if they use many terms for profit.

I figured calculating the EBITDA for Tesla might be fun, because that's me. You can find the 10-K for Tesla on the web. They don't put their financial statements in their annual report, probably because Tesla shareholders don't really give a shit about the actual finances of the company. That's my take.

In Tesla's 2023 10-K, which is the SEC name for an annual report, you'll find the "Consolidated Statements of Operations" on page 50, which is akin to an income statement, as far as I can tell. It's got all the familiar line items with a half dozen different ways to say the same thing. Here's my summary.

	Lots of Money[80]
Revenue	96,773
Cost of revenues	-79,113
Gross profit	**17,660**
Operating Expenses	-8,769
Income from operations	**8,891**
Interest income	1,066
Interest expense	-156
Other net income	172
Income before tax	**9,973**
Tax provision (this is +)	-5,001
Net Income	**14,974**

At least these guys used only two words, **profit** and **income**, to define all the bits left after expenses are peeled away from revenue.

But, you ask, where is depreciation? Good question. I asked the same thing, but I said it to myself because I was alone while I wrote this and it was kind of creepy. Like most financial statements, there were a ton of warnings that "The

---

[80] Carl Sagan should have been referenced here, but the numbers are in millions, not billions.

accompanying notes are an integral part of these consolidated financial statements."

Within the notes, if you search for "depreciation" you find that depreciation for Tesla is included in the cost of sales and doesn't appear on the income statement. You can find it on the cash flow statement on page 53. It is 4,337.

So, our **EBITDA** is Earnings (14,974) before Interest (910), Taxes (-5,001) and Depreciation (4,337):   **15,220**.

Now, if you search online for Tesla's EBITDA for 2024, you'll find a different number. It's not too different, but it's different. And this is because of some analyst, somewhere, saw an item in the notes and decided it was an atypical item and should be removed from a calculation of the company's EBITDA, or available cash for financing and other fun.

And that's fine. Financial numbers are not exact when dealing in the billions. Plus, Tesla has massive payouts to executives and lawsuits and all kinds of craziness that makes a straightforward EBITDA calculation just another data point, not the whole story. EBITDA might not even be very useful for a company like Tesla. I mean, really, is anyone buying this stock based on annual trailing metrics?

A Note On Notes

If you were an accounting firm and had to put your reputation (and potential fines and jail time) on the line when submitting audited financial statements for your clients to the SEC, banks, the shareholders, and the public, you might want to add some caveats. These are the Notes that Accompany the Financial Statements.

Like the Tesla financial statements, where I had to hunt within the notes to find depreciation, the notes to any audited financial statement elucidate and inform. Without the notes, you really might be reading the back of a *Cap'n Crunch* box, not the income statement of a trillion-dollar company. Notes have all the stuff that the company really, really wants to hide, but cannot legally do so. Or stuff that's really boring. Or both. Good luck on that.

In particular, notes are good for those one-time items that can really change a metric like EBITDA. Say there's accelerated amortization of some acquisition. That'll be in the notes. Without reading the notes, you'd estimate wrong. And your EBITDA calculation would be wrong. And you'd get fired and have to learn welding or something.

Some Stuff on Financial Modeling

Financial models are used to *predict* financial performance. Therefore, they are closer to necromancy than accounting (which is more like necrophilia than golf). Predicting the future is the goal, which tells you why it's so important to use some rational techniques.

Nobody can predict the future, but that's what we are trying to do. And by understanding some methods for doing that, we will also learn how to analyze the past. It's all very *Eastern philosophy* and might even help you avoid therapy.

When you are building a financial model, you'll probably start with the income statement. That isn't really very logical. If you were analyzing your own life, you'd probably start with your balance sheet: What do I own? Whom do I owe? And most accounting books and teaching methods start with the *equation* that represents the balance sheet of an organization.

But financial modeling is generally done for projecting a business, and businesses are all about selling. Selling is captured on the income statement.

Spreadsheet-based financial models are designed to be read left to right. Time periods are on the x-axis moving from current (left) to future (right). Rows of financial data travel downward, each cell adding to the information of the row above it and to the left, resulting in summary information at the bottom. Like so:

	A	B	C	D	E	F	G	H
			Year 1	Year 2	Year 3	...Year N		
2	Revenue		input	=c2	input	=b(n-1)		
3	Costs	constant	input	=c2*(1+b3)	=d3*(1+b3)	etc.		
4	Profit		=c2-c3	=d2-d3	=e2-e3			
5								
6	...again with numbers							
7								
8	Revenue		500.00	500.00	600.00	600.00		
9	Costs	8%	400.00	432.00	466.56	503.88		
10	Profit		100.00	68.00	133.44	96.12		
11								

TIP: Blue cells. This is a trick I got from AGWAMBA.[81] Some cells are the result of calculations; some cells are real numbers that you have typed into the cell. Cells with real numbers are called inputs, and I make all inputs blue. You can use whatever color you want. If you do this, you'll have a much easier time reading your model, like at midnight when your investment presentation is due at 8 a.m. the next day, or if you put down your model and don't look at it again for many months. There are tutorials on the interwebs on how to automate this.

TIP: Set up your rows so that there is a constant column

---

[81] AGWAMBA—a guy with an MBA. In fact, that guy is John, a friend of mine who always made the most awesome financial models.

and an initial input. Cells for later months are simply equal to the earlier months plus your constant function. Your constant could be a percentage increase (as in the example above). This is a useful way to set up your cells. This way, if you want to type a specific number into a cell, such as year 3 revenue, above, all the following cells take on that new value. You can type in a specific change and it's automatically carried through the future months or years. Remember to make that input cell blue or you won't be able to find it later.

TIP: To hide a cell without affecting its contents, set the color of the font to white.

Your model can be for a single quarter (three months) or for 50 years. I worked for many years in the timber investment business, and 30-year models were standard since trees take so long to grow.

However, the value of the model's predictions beyond, say, five years is very low; some will say that limit is more like two years. People can't predict how much money they'll have in their own personal checking accounts week to week. Do you think you can predict the financial state of a company 10 years from now? Not bloody likely.

It is physically difficult to read a model with hundreds of columns, yet I've seen folks try to present this type of model to venture capitalists.

Generally, don't make a weekly model for more than a year. Don't make a monthly model for more than three years. Don't make a quarterly model for more than five years. I think weekly models are not very valuable. There's too much error in a weekly prediction. If you are modeling a start-up company, it might have some value, but monthly is probably your best bet.

I generally made two-year, month-to-month models for start-ups. Most analyst reports include a quarter-to-quarter projection for two years. I never liked quarters because I have trouble thinking in "quarters," though the financial community relies heavily on quarter-to-quarter comparisons.

How Do I Model Stock Options?

Answer: You can't. Stock options suck from a modeling perspective, particularly out-of-the-money ones.[82] They aren't entitled to a share of earnings. They aren't even shares of the company. Really they are contracts with the company, not equity and not debt. If they are in the money, especially if they are substantially in the money, you could assume they will get exercised and simply convert them to equity in your model. Be aware, though, that if they then go out of the money, your model will be wrong.

With some options, because they are very likely to get exercised (for instance if they'll expire otherwise), you should exercise them in your model just before expiration, add the proceeds to your cash-from-financing area, and increase the equity on the balance sheet, just as if the company had a planned sale of shares.

---

[82] An out-of-the-money option is one in which the strike price is above the current price. So if you give your employee an option to buy one share at $10 and the current price is $5 per share, then the option is out of the money. This refers to call options, which are options to buy stock. Put options are options to sell stock.

Cool Ways To Make Money

To end this book, I'll just toss out some very simple ways that companies play with accounting to rob, cheat and steal from anyone at all.[83]

Off-Balance-Sheet Financing

This is neato torpedo stuff and pretty simple. I'll give an example of a very popular off-balance-sheet financing called a *sale-leaseback*.

Let's say your company owns an office building and occupies it. On your balance sheet is something like this:

Balance Sheet

Assets	
1 Main Street building	2,000,000
Minus accumulated depreciation	500,000
Total assets	1,500,000
Liabilities (mortgage)	1,000,000

Your mortgage and taxes on the building are $15,000 per

---

[83] "When elephants fight, the grass is trampled." – African proverb

month.

It turns out that your head of procurement was sleeping with one of your vendors and bought $500,000 worth of toilet paper just before taking early retirement. You need some cash fast.

You sell the building for $1.5 million (book value) and lease it back from the seller for, say, $18,000 per month.

Your balance now looks like this:

Balance Sheet

Assets	
cash	500,000
Liabilities	zilch

Ah, the wonders of accounting. Now, for the minor cost of $3,000 extra per month, you've paid off your cash shortage. What's the financial difference for the company? Just an increased payment. And, in fact, you reported $1.5 million in cash flow from the sale of the building, none of which was taxable since it was sold for book value. The company is completely different on Wall Street. Now it has "no debt," "strong cash flow," and a "strong balance sheet." Really, it's actually in a worse financial position because its rental obligations are greater than previously.

You can do this with any asset. In fact, here's a good trick: Find a company with lots of assets. Buy it and make yourself CEO. Sell all the assets and lease them all back. Report freakin' high cash flow to Wall Street. When the stock rallies, sell your stock. Now, as CEO take that buckus-load of cash you have on the balance sheet and pay yourself a huge, womping bonus. Retire. Ignore the screams in two years when the company runs out of cash and has no assets.

Think I'm kidding? Read the *Wall Street Journal*.

High Cash Flow—No Profit

Here's a great trick. In fact, it's less a trick than standard operating procedure at many companies.

Ideally, you've gotten some idea from this tutorial about the difference between cash flow and profit. As a quick recap, cash flow is what's coming in minus what's going out. Profit is all the revenue minus the expenses, but includes non-cash charges. Key is that cash flow can be measured as just cash from operations or can include cash from financing and/or cash from investing.

If you sell shares, your cash flow will rise. In fact, if you sell an asset, your cash flow will rise.

So just sell shares and spend all your time selling shares and forget about profit. Investors love "cash flow." Profit is for ninnies. Cash flow is for real businessmen anyway. This is also called a Ponzi scheme, but let's not put too many labels on stuff, mmm-kay?

Enron

Enron did lots of cool stuff. Some of which was probably legal. I have no actual knowledge of Enron or its partnerships, but based on what I've gotten from the press, I think they did something like this, among other things:

They formed a partnership—let's call it Partnership A. They went around to investors and sold units in Partnership A. Partnership A then took that money and lent it to Enron.

Partnership A was considered an Enron subsidiary. Therefore, the debt between Partnership A and Enron didn't need to be explicitly listed on the Enron balance sheet. This is called "consolidating" and is a great way to hide debt, kind of like if your mother lent you $5,000 and then someone asked you if you had any debt, you'd say no since the intra-familial rule of accounting is that you don't have to report money your mother lends you.

However, to make things better, Enron agreed to repay Partnership A by offering Enron shares as collateral. If Enron shares declined, Partnership A would simply receive more of them.

Since this worked well in 1999, they did it again, in a bigger way, in 2000. And so on.

Apparently, by the time Enron declared bankruptcy, the number of shares the Partnership was entitled to was a significant percentage of Enron.

Avoid Taxes—Go to the Beach!

Simply move your parent company to a place with low corporate taxes (Cayman Islands, anyone?) and recognize all your revenue there. Leave all your expenses in the place with high corporate taxes.

Pumping Earnings by Losing Money

Strange but true! (This really happened, perhaps, maybe.) Let's say you are IBM. You buy Lotus Software for some multibillion-dollar number. After buying a big company, normally you would put the, say, $3.5 billion purchase price on your balance sheet and amortize it over several years, taking a non-cash charge each year to reflect the multiyear nature of the cost. This would reduce your earnings per share in the future, but you wouldn't have to recognize a big cost all at once from the acquisition.

But if the market is crappy and lots of companies are taking big charges, you could, instead, take one *whopping* charge against earnings the year you bought Lotus, assuming you've made enough campaign donations to make sure the SEC doesn't care. In future years there's no amortization, resulting in higher earnings per share. Make sure you issue stock options to all the senior execs when the stock tanks after you take that giant hit. (I don't know if IBM actually did that.)

Afterword

There's a decent financial model available for free on wtfisebitda.com. It even has a depreciation worksheet and a loan worksheet. Enjoy.

I have nothing more to add. Well, I probably do, but I want to publish this before I die, so you'll have to live with this crappy sign-off.

About the Author

Steven Saltman is a former stock options trader, internet entrepreneur and investment banker. He is the author of *Diagnosis + 6 Days*, one of the least popular books on Amazon.

In no particular order, he has sailed across the Pacific, earned a master's degree in forestry economics, founded and sold a tech company, been in an Oscar-winning movie, worked in a top-secret nuclear laboratory, served in the US Peace Corps (Lesotho) and run several marathons. Many years ago he was chosen as one of Boston's "40 Under 40."

If you liked this book, please leave a review.

Wishing you the best,
Steve